D1327914

The Little Book of
Egyptian Hieroglyphs

The Little Book of

Egyptian Hieroglyphs

LESLEY AND ROY ADKINS

Hodder & Stoughton

Copyright © 2001 by Lesley and Roy Adkins

First published in Great Britain in 2001 by Hodder and Stoughton
A division of Hodder Headline

The right of Lesley and Roy Adkins to be identified as the Author of the Work has been asserted by them
in accordance with the Copyright, Designs and Patents Act 1988.

10 9 8 7 6 5 4 3 2 1

A CIP catalogue record for this title is available from the British Library.

ISBN 0 340 79485 2

Typeset in Minion by Nigel Strudwick
Hieroglyphic fonts by Cleo Huggins

Printed and bound in Great Britain by
Mackays of Chatham plc, Chatham, Kent

Hodder and Stoughton
A division of Hodder Headline
338 Euston Road
London NW1 3BH

To Clare, Robert, Ella and Sophie, with love

Acknowledgements

In the writing of this book we are indebted to Rowena Webb, Rosemary Trapnell and Emma Heyworth-Dunn at Hodder & Stoughton and to Morag Lyall for the copy-editing. We are also grateful to Nigel Strudwick for his invaluable advice and for his typesetting. We would also like to thank 𓊪𓄿𓏤𓏏𓇋𓄿 𓇋𓄿𓋴𓏏.

Contents

Contents

A Little Introduction

Hieroglyphs, the writing of ancient Egypt, have been around for thousands of years. They are fascinating to look at, because many of the signs are recognisable as pictures of people 𓀀, 𓀭, 𓀎, 𓂝, parts of the body 𓂀, 𓂐, animals 𓃮, 𓃒, 𓃞, 𓃭, birds 𓅂, 𓅆, 𓅸, fish 𓆜, insects 𓆣, and plants 𓆰, while others seem at first glance positively strange 𓈖, 𓊪, 𓎼, 𓏏, 𓊃, 𓏤, 𓂋.

Put together in rows and columns, these hieroglyphic symbols form an infinite variety of patterns that were an important part of ancient Egyptian art. Some can be written quite simply, while others are minor masterpieces in themselves, but these hieroglyphs were not just pictures: to those who could read them, they were a sophisticated system of writing used for accounts, historical records, stories, love poetry and, above all, magic spells. Today hieroglyphs are found in huge numbers carved and often painted in bright colours on the walls of temples and tombs in Egypt, as well as on many objects such as coffins, statues, papyri, pottery vessels and mummy bandages in museums all over the world.

Along with the pyramids and sphinx, hieroglyphs are the most easily recognised symbol of ancient Egypt, and some of them, such as ☥ (the ankh, a symbol of life), are now so frequently used as charms and pendants that their origins are sometimes forgotten. The ankh sign is made up of a T-shape with a loop on top and may have depicted the strap of a simple sandal, with the loop going round the ankle. It came to be a symbol of life on earth and of eternal life and was adopted as the sign of the cross by the later Coptic Christian Church in Egypt.

There are thousands of Egyptian hieroglyphs, although around 500 of them were much more commonly used than the others. Even so, the thought of learning to read hieroglyphs can be daunting. The aim of this book is to give a very straightforward introduction for anyone first encountering hieroglyphs – for students, for tourists wanting to get more out of their trip to Egypt, and for anyone interested in ancient Egypt and ancient languages. This is not an academic, scholarly book, but it is intended to make hieroglyphs enjoyable to read.

The first part of the book gives short explanations of the history of Egypt's language and writing systems, the decipherment of hieroglyphs after the ability to read them had been lost, and how scribes wrote and what they wrote. The workings of hieroglyphs are covered next, with explanations of their different functions, vowels, punctuation, the direction of writing, pronunciation, and how hieroglyphs are written out in English ('transliteration'). The most commonly used hieroglyphs are then dealt with, and many can be used in the following section on how to write your own name. Delving a little further into grammar, we also take a look at plurals, numbers, gender, verbs, genitives and pronouns, ending by analysing a few words.

In the next section hieroglyphs are looked at in relation to names. For the pharaohs, a list of their reigns is given as an introduction, and then explanations of their names, followed by several commonly encountered pharaohs, with their names given in hieroglyphs and translation. Words and names in hieroglyphs are also given in the descriptions of what the ancient Egyptians thought about time and the seasons, eternal life after death, and gods and goddesses. A few place names will perhaps assist the planning of a trip to Egypt, while for anyone pursuing hieroglyphs further, some phrases are explained and recommendations given on how to study hieroglyphs and ancient Egypt in greater detail.

Few people visit Egypt without bringing back their name in hieroglyphs on a gold pendant or a piece of papyrus. The ancient Egyptians had an easy way of writing names of foreigners in hieroglyphs, so at the very least this book will enable you to do the same today. But be warned: Egypt and its hieroglyphs can be addictive. You may just get hooked.

A Little History

Oldest Writing System

Hieroglyphs were first used for writing the ancient Egyptian language at least 5,000 years ago. Archaeologists still argue over whether the earliest examples of writing in the world are Egyptian hieroglyphs or a script found in Iraq known as cuneiform. Recent finds in Egypt of primitive symbols dating to about 3500 BC have swayed the argument in favour of hieroglyphs.

Spoken Language

Only one language was written in hieroglyphs: the language of ancient Egyptian, with its different dialects up and down the Nile Valley. The ancient Egyptian language lasted for over 4,000 years, and during that time it underwent many changes, just as languages do today. The English that was in use 600 years ago, such as that written by Chaucer, is very different from what is spoken and written today and can be very difficult to understand, although it is still recognisable as English. It is therefore not difficult to imagine the many changes to the Egyptian language that occurred over 4,000 years.

Hieroglyphs cannot be understood without knowing the Egyptian language. Even when writing developed in Egypt, most people would not have been able to read and write, but they still spoke ancient Egyptian. This is now a dead language, but it was related to Asiatic ('Semitic') languages such as Arabic and Hebrew and also to North African ('Hamitic') languages such as Berber. Much of the difficulty in reading hieroglyphs comes from the fact that not only does a different script need to be learned, with a large number of strange symbols, but the ancient Egyptian language has to be coped with as well.

For convenience, Egyptologists divide the ancient Egyptian language into various stages. Old Egyptian was probably being spoken before 3000 BC, but this is uncertain because the earliest writing only consists of simple lists and labels. It was definitely being spoken by 2600 BC and lasted for around 500 years.

From 2100 BC Middle Egyptian (which is also called Classical Egyptian) was spoken, again for a period of about 500 years. Middle Egyptian was closely related to Old Egyptian in its structure. From 1600 BC Late Egyptian began to replace Middle Egyptian as the everyday spoken language, and was very different, especially in its grammar. Middle Egyptian did not die out, as it continued to be the formal language used in literary texts and inscriptions right up to the Roman period, even though it was no longer the everyday language of the people.

Around 650 BC Late Egyptian developed into what is now called demotic, and this became the everyday language: the word 'demotic' derives from the ancient Greek word for 'popular'. The Greek-speaking Alexander the Great conquered Egypt in 332 BC, and from that period ancient Greek itself became the official administrative language and the spoken language of many of the nobility, alongside demotic. This was the first time that two distinct languages were spoken side by side in Egypt, whereas the transition from Old Egyptian through Middle Egyptian to Late Egyptian would have been smooth and gradual, with no overlaps in the spoken language.

When the Romans took over Egypt in 30 BC, its defeated Queen Cleopatra committed suicide and Egypt became part of the Roman Empire. In western Europe, Latin was the main spoken language of the Roman Empire, but as the Romans expanded their empire eastwards into what had been the ancient Greek world of Greece, Cyprus, Turkey and beyond, the Greek language continued to be used. Although Greek remained the language of administration in Egypt, demotic continued to be spoken by most people.

The final phase of ancient Egyptian was Coptic, which developed in the Roman period from around AD 100. 'Copt' is a modern word that simply means 'Egyptian' – a corruption of *qubti*, the Arabic form of the ancient Greek word *Aigyptos*, meaning Egypt. Coptic was closely related to demotic and was spoken for over 1,000 years. Even though the Arabic language was introduced in the seventh century AD (with the Arab invasion of Egypt), it was not until the fifteenth century AD that Coptic finally died out as a spoken language. It is still used in the Coptic Christian Church in Egypt in the same way that Latin is used in the Roman Catholic Church.

While the ancient Egyptian language changed gradually over the centuries, at any one time there would undoubtedly have been different dialects, as occur in languages today: the pronunciation of a language and even its vocabulary can vary between regions, such as the different types of English spoken in southern England, north-east England, Scotland and America. It is not possible to recognise dialects in ancient Egyptian until it developed into Coptic, when the main dialects are called Sahidic and Bohairic.

Written Language

The written language of the ancient Egyptians was slower to develop than the spoken language. Hieroglyphs were used to write down the Old and Middle Egyptian language, but not Late Egyptian. Although Late Egyptian began to replace Middle Egyptian as the spoken language from around 1600 BC, hieroglyphs continued to be used to write Middle Egyptian, which survived for another 1,500 years. Middle Egyptian continued as the written formal language for funerary, religious and monumental inscriptions. It is Middle Egyptian that is most commonly studied today.

Hieroglyphs were a kind of formal writing, equivalent to the texts in medieval illuminated manuscripts, or nowadays to carved inscriptions on monuments (such as on tombstones and war memorials) and printed text in books. Hieroglyphs could be very elaborate, even detailing the feathers on a bird, and many were also painted, although the colours do not always survive today.

Hieroglyphs were not the only way to write the Egyptian language. A handwriting (cursive, or flowing) form of hieroglyphs known as hieratic developed from around 2600 BC. The writing of hieroglyphs was too cumbersome for everyday purposes, and a much faster method of handwriting was needed. Hieratic was written with a reed pen and ink (usually black ink, sometimes with red highlights), mainly on papyrus but also on other surfaces such as broken pieces of pottery. It was used for writing Old, Middle and Late Egyptian.

Hieratic writing changed in style over the centuries, and the different styles can be used to estimate when a text was written. In hieratic, the hieroglyphic signs became much less pictorial, and some were replaced altogether by more simple signs. Hieratic could be 'joined-up' writing, with two or more signs joined with lines called ligatures. Because hieratic is a simplified version of hieroglyphs, it is possible to convert the writing into the equivalent hieroglyphic signs. Most students begin by learning hieroglyphs rather than hieratic, but the first step towards reading hieratic texts often involves this conversion exercise.

Linear hieroglyphs (also called cursive hieroglyphs) were individual hieroglyphs drawn in ink with a reed pen in outline form only, in a single colour, mainly on papyri and coffins. They were simplified hieroglyphs, slower to write than hieratic and as such were considered more distinguished than hieratic for temple manuscripts and funerary texts. They were mainly written in vertical columns. In modern terms, linear hieroglyphs were 'calligraphy', used on important documents rather than hieratic 'handwriting'.

Late Egyptian hieratic writing became very stylised, developing into the script known today as demotic. The demotic writing system does not resemble hieroglyphs, and so it is not converted into hieroglyphs to study the texts. Demotic began to replace hieratic from around 650 BC, especially for business documents. It was written mainly on papyri, with pen and ink, although it was also increasingly used for monumental inscriptions because by now very few people could understand hieroglyphs. Consequently, the Rosetta Stone, which was set up at this time, had an inscription in three different languages (Middle Egyptian, demotic and ancient Greek), so that everyone who was likely to see it would understand it. The modern equivalent is setting up a monument in Wales with an inscription repeated in Latin, Welsh and English. Demotic began to die out in the third century AD, and the last known inscription was carved at Philae in AD 452.

From the time of Alexander the Great's conquest in 332 BC, many bureaucratic texts were also written in Greek and continued to be so right through the Roman period. At the same time the Coptic script developed towards the end of the first century AD, primarily for writing down the translations of Christian texts into the Egyptian language. Although the Coptic language developed from demotic, Coptic writing is completely different from hieroglyphs, hieratic and demotic. Instead, it was greatly influenced by Greek, and consists of the letters of the Greek alphabet (consonants and vowels) along with a few demotic characters to express some peculiarly Egyptian sounds.

The development of writing in ancient Egypt can be seen in the owl hieroglyph (the letter 'm'). At times it could be a very ornate hieroglyph, with details such as feathers being shown.

A more simple form is

with the equivalent cursive hieroglyph appearing as

the hieratic symbol as

the demotic as or

and the Coptic as .

Hieroglyphs went out of use during the Roman period, as by then this form of writing was mainly confined to scribes in temples, and the writing system could not survive the closure of the pagan temples by the Romans. The last dated hieroglyphic inscription was carved in stone at Philae on 24 August AD 394. By the end of the fifth century AD, Coptic was the only means of writing the Egyptian language, for both Christian and non-religious purposes. The skills needed to write hieroglyphs were lost, and hieroglyphs could no longer be understood.

Decipherment

Egypt was closed to the western world for centuries, and only a few explorers and merchants managed to visit the country during this time. In 1798 all that changed, because Napoleon Bonaparte and his French army invaded Egypt. Over 150 scholars and scientists accompanied his expedition, and they were amazed to discover so many ancient ruins, still covered with hieroglyphs.

In 1799 the Rosetta Stone was discovered, which had three inscriptions: one in demotic script (written in the demotic language and probably the first of the three inscriptions to be written) and then approximate versions in hieroglyphs (in the Middle Egyptian language) and in the ancient Greek script (in the ancient Greek language). This discovery gave enormous encouragement to attempts to decipher the now mysterious hieroglyphs. In England a doctor called Thomas Young made great progress, but he was rapidly overtaken by a young French scholar called Jean-François Champollion who was obsessed with ancient languages and with Egypt. Champollion had become fluent in Coptic, the very last stage of ancient Egyptian, and this helped him enormously in his studies. In 1822 he announced that he had made a huge discovery and at last hieroglyphs could be deciphered. This was only the beginning of the study of hieroglyphs, as there was so much to learn, and new ideas are being developed and new discoveries are still being made today.

What Are Hieroglyphs?

Hieroglyphs are ancient Egyptian writing signs that in many cases appear to be pictures or diagrams, such as 🦅 (a man hiding behind a wall) and ◊ (an egg). When Champollion deciphered hieroglyphs, he thought there were 864 different signs in total, but today it is thought that the earliest hieroglyphs numbered about 1,000, decreasing to about 750 around 2000 BC and increasing to several thousand in Ptolemaic Greek and Roman times. There were only ever about 500 signs that were very commonly used.

With so many signs it is impossible to learn them in the same way as the English alphabet, because there are far too many to memorise and recall in the same way that children recite their a, b, c. Another system to classify and put them in some sort of order had to be invented. In 1927 Sir Alan Gardiner, a British Egyptologist, published the first edition of *Egyptian Grammar. Being an Introduction to the Study of Hieroglyphs*, which is one of the most important works ever to be published on hieroglyphs. In this book, he classified the hieroglyphic signs by subject matter, giving each one a unique number. For example, section D of his list is 'Parts of the Human Body', in which D1 ◈ is a head, D2 ◈ is a face, D18 𝄐 is an ear, and so on, while section F is 'Parts of Mammals', with F13 ∪

representing horns and F31 ⚏ depicting three fox skins tied together.

Some of the hieroglyph pictures that seem obscure today, such as N34 ⌒ (an ingot of metal) and N23 ⌗ (an irrigation canal), have been identified by means of careful study of many inscriptions and by an in-depth knowledge of life in ancient Egypt. Someone looking up the meaning of a hieroglyph, though, may not themselves be familiar with its identification, but Gardiner also grouped the signs according to their shape. So an unfamiliar sign such as ⚘ can be looked up in his table of vertical signs, where it is identified as S35; this is actually the sign of a fan or sunshade. Similarly, the sign ⌐ can be searched for under horizontal signs, where it is identified as U19; this is a picture of an adze.

Gardiner's numbering system is universally used today by Egyptologists, who are quite familiar, for example, with the terms O9 and S24. The system is used in books published on hieroglyphs and in computer programs used for composing texts in hieroglyphs. It is important as a universal method of classification and is an invaluable source of information for students and scholars. To find out about the sign ⌐, for example, Gardiner's classification would number this as I10 and say that it depicts a cobra, but represents the sound 'dj'. There are several similar signs such as ⌣ (Gardiner number I9), ⚘ (Gardiner number I11), ⚘ (Gardiner number I12) and ⌣ (Gardiner number I14), so his method avoids confusion and provides an indispensable reference for Egyptologists worldwide.

'Hieroglyph', by the way, is a noun. The word 'hieroglyphic' is an adjective and should not be used as a noun. The correct usage is: hieroglyphs and hieroglyphic signs.

The Role of the Scribe

Training

It is not known exactly how many people could read and write in ancient Egypt. Probably only about 1 per cent of the population may have been able to write, although a few more may have been able to read, but not write, while others may have been able to read and write a few words only. Ninety-nine per cent of the population were therefore illiterate. This figure is still a matter of debate among Egyptologists, because numerous examples of writing have been found in excavated villages, such as Deir El-Medina at Thebes, where the builders of the tombs in the Valley of the Kings lived.

The people who were trained to read and write – the scribes (from the Latin word *scribere*, 'to write') – were privileged, high-status members of society. To be a scribe was something special. Men who held important jobs or who were nobles considered it prestigious to be depicted as scribes, even if they had never been one: many statues survive of such people, who are shown sitting with their legs crossed, a papyrus unrolled on their lap, and sometimes holding a pen.

Most scribes were trained to write hieratic – the handwriting form of hieroglyphs – and probably never even progressed to writing hieroglyphs. Many worked in temples, and their prime function would have been to write documents on papyrus rolls in hieratic writing. Training at schools included the laborious copying of literary texts in hieratic and cursive hieroglyphs, often on to fragments of broken pottery and limestone chippings, rather than waste good papyrus. Mistakes are visible on these practice pieces, and teachers are known to have beaten their pupils as punishment.

Writing Materials

Hieroglyphs were mainly carved into the stone walls of temples and tombs. They were also carved and/or painted on other objects of stone (such as sarcophagi, statues and stelae), as well as on things made from other materials such as wooden coffins and glazed tiles. Cursive hieroglyphs were written mainly on papyrus rolls and wooden coffins, and hieratic was commonly written on papyrus and on pieces of stone and pottery, some of which were extremely large.

Papyrus

A roll of papyrus was known as ![glyph] , 'shefedu'. Papyrus was a type of paper made from the tall papyrus plant (*Cyperus papyrus*) that once grew abundantly in the still, shallow waters of the Egyptian marshlands. The plant was used to make a variety of things from sandals and baskets to river boats. For the manufacture of 'paper', the stem of the plant was used. After harvesting, the stems were cut to the required length and the outer skin or rind was peeled off. The core of the stem was then cut or peeled into strips, which were laid side by side and another layer of strips placed on top, at right angles to the first layer. The two layers were then pressed or beaten together, and the natural adhesives in the plant welded the strips together as they dried out. The result was a sheet of papyrus, slightly thicker than modern writing paper, that was ready for the scribe to use.

Pens and Ink

For many purposes a scribe would use a palette, often made of wood, which had a slot with a sliding cover designed to hold a few pens, as well as having holes for the cakes of black and red ink. This set of equipment was called ⊟ ▢ ▦, 'menhed'.

The last hieroglyph, ▦, is a picture of the scribal equipment, used here as a determinative (see page 31), which could also be used as the sign for 'sesh', meaning a 'scribe' and 'to write'. The equipment as shown in the hieroglyph is a palette, a bag or pot for water (or possibly for pigments) and a case for pens, all held together by a cord. In practice, the pens were often stored in the palette.

Pens were made from reeds, the ends of which were frayed (often by chewing), to form something more like a brush than a nib. Pointed reed pens were only introduced into Egypt by the Greeks in the third century BC.

Black ink (made of carbon black, usually soot) was most commonly used on papyri, with red ink (made from ochre) being reserved for highlighting particular sections (such as totals of numbers, headings and dates), but other colours were used for illustrations in more ornate texts. The inks were made into solid cakes, which were not used as a liquid; instead, the scribe dipped the pen in water and rubbed it on a cake of ink, in much the same way as watercolour paints are used today.

Divine Writing

To the ancient Egyptians, writing was a gift from the gods. The god Thoth was believed to have invented writing and so he was the main god of writing, as well as being a god of dates and the measurement of time. Seshat was a goddess of writing, as well as of accounts and measurements.

In ancient Egyptian, the name for hieroglyphs was 'god's words' or 'divine speech', ⊓|, 'medu-neter', and words were believed to be very powerful, especially in magic and ritual. Amulets were worn by people and placed on mummies to bring good luck or keep away evil, and many were in the shape of particular hieroglyphs. The Eye of Horus, ⟨ ('wedjat'), acted as a protective device in amulets and jewellery, while millions of amulets were made in the shape of ⟨, the scarab beetle, a symbol of eternal life and resurrection.

The ankh, ⚲, became a powerful amulet of eternal life, and the djed pillar, ⨅, became a symbol of long life and stability. A common group of hieroglyphs used as a magic formula or amulet was ⚲⎜⎜, 'ankh udja s', an abbreviation for 'ankh udja seneb' meaning 'life, prosperity and health'. Another combination of hieroglyphs was ⚲⨅⎜, 'ankh djed was'. The 'was' hieroglyph, ⎜, was an animal-headed staff that was carried by the gods. This hieroglyph represented the sound 'was', meaning power, and was sometimes depicted with arms and hands. Another protective device was the hieroglyph ⌒, whose shape was used to surround and protect the throne name and birth name of pharaohs (see page 96).

It was believed that in some circumstances representations such as statues, pictures and even hieroglyphs could come to life. If such representations were of dangerous things, fierce animals or known enemies, an effort was made to neutralise the danger. In funerary texts that were carved and painted on walls and written on papyrus, the threat to the dead person from dangerous hieroglyphs was lessened by writing them in the unlucky colour red or by showing them pierced with spears or knives. This was done, for example, to groups of hieroglyphs such as ꝏ, the name of Apophis, the snake god of the underworld.

What They Wrote

Even though only a small fraction of the writings of ancient Egypt in hieroglyphs and hieratic ('handwriting') has survived, it nevertheless represents a huge range, from formal, monumental inscriptions carved on temple walls to graffiti scratched on broken pottery fragments. There are sets of accounts (such as lists of agricultural produce), king lists (lists of pharaohs with their length of reign), lists of historical events, deeds of sale, tax documents, census lists, royal decrees, technical texts (primarily on medicine and mathematics, and containing practical examples), military despatches, inscriptions on statues, commemorative inscriptions, funerary spells, religious rituals and hymns, funerary autobiographies in tombs, records of military campaigns, letters (private and business), wisdom texts (moralising set texts copied out by apprentice scribes) and narrative tales. Apart from the lack of theatrical plays and possibly non-religious songs (although some of the poetry may have been sung), the ancient Egyptians used writing for the same purposes as it is used today, as well as for additional ones, such as writing letters to the dead which were posted in tombs.

Many texts are believed to have been written in verse form, not prose form, but Egyptologists argue about this. Magic spells for the protection of the dead and for survival in the next world (the after-life) are the largest single group of surviving writing in Egypt, the most important of which are the Pyramid Texts, Coffin Texts and Book of the Dead. The attempts to make these spells durable, so that they would be effective for as long as possible, resulted in more copies of such spells surviving than any other Egyptian literature.

To ensure the survival of the dead pharaoh in the afterlife, spells were recited by his relatives and priests, but in case they failed to perform the rituals, steps were taken to give a more permanent existence to the spells. From around 2300 BC, the spells were inscribed in hieroglyphs on the walls of the chambers inside the pyramids where the pharaohs were buried. It was believed that as long as the hieroglyphs survived, the spells would remain effective for the pharaoh. These particular spells are now known as Pyramid Texts.

Around 2000 BC these spells began to be inscribed in the tombs of the nobles and their families as well as in the tombs of the phar-aohs. The nobles had now also begun to seek survival after death through mummification and magic spells. Previously, they had tried to be buried as close as possible to the pharaoh's tomb, hoping to share in his resurrection. The wording of the spells used by the nobles was similar to that of the Pyramid Texts, but with some alterations and omissions. Rather than being written on the walls of the tombs, they were written on wooden coffins and for that reason are called Coffin Texts.

About 500 years later spells now known as the Book of the Dead began to replace the Coffin Texts. Rather than being a book with specific contents, the Book of the Dead is actually a collection of about 200 spells, prayers and hymns, many derived from the Pyramid Texts and Coffin Texts. Different surviving copies of the Book of the Dead contain varying sets of spells. They were no longer written on the coffin, but on a roll of papyrus (hence the term 'book'), which was buried in the tomb or inside the coffin. The modern title of Book of the Dead is misleading, as the ancient Egyptian view of these collections of spells was closer to Book of Living Forever or Book of Resurrection.

Transliteration

When Jean-François Champollion began to decipher hieroglyphs and hieratic, his success was partly due to his practice of trying to match the signs with the later Coptic writing and convert them into Coptic. He was then able to see if a Coptic word existed that was fairly similar to his ancient Egyptian word, and because Champollion was fluent in Coptic, he could translate the word into his own language of French. He therefore went through the following stages: hieroglyphs => Coptic writing => Coptic word => French. Although this was an excellent way to start decipherment, it was not always an accurate method, because the language had of course changed greatly over thousands of years. This problem can be seen today, for example, in languages that have descended from Latin: the Latin word for 'four' is *quattuor*, but in French it has changed to *quatre*, while the Latin for 'eagle' is *aquila*, but the French word has changed to *aigle*.

Today hieroglyphs are *transliterated* or converted into a set of alphabetical symbols that can be understood by Egyptologists in many parts of the world. The word 'transliterate', which is derived from the Latin words *trans* ('across', or 'over') and *littera* ('letter'), is the process of converting the letters of one alphabet into the letters of another. The words can then be translated into other languages, such as English, German or Dutch.

This sounds quite a straightforward process, but there are three major problems: the lack of punctuation in hieroglyphs (see page 33), the lack of vowels in hieroglyphs (see page 34), and the modern alphabet into which the hieroglyphs are converted. Because the European alphabet is pronounced in different ways in different countries ('j' and 'w' are pronounced differently in Germany and England, for example), a special universal alphabet was devised in the late nineteenth century to represent the Egyptian sounds, including some letters with diacritics or accents (signs above or below the letter), which can change the pronunciation of a letter radically. This system can be very difficult for anyone just starting to learn hieroglyphs, because this special alphabet also has to be learned!

To make things more straightforward, the transliteration alphabet is not used in this book, but a simplified system is used instead. For example, the word ⌐ ⌐ ✕ ⌐ , meaning 'to teach', should be transliterated as *sbꜣ*. To make this easier to pronounce, a vowel is inserted between the 's' and 'b', and the final symbol is better understood if written as 'a', and so the transliteration used in this book is 'seba'. Another example is ⌐ ⌐ ⌐ , meaning 'beer'. The transliteration should be *ḥnqt*, but *ḥ* is a harsh 'h', and no vowels are shown. In this book the word is transliterated as 'henqet'. The word ⌐ ⌐ , meaning 'harvest', should be transliterated as *šmw*. In this book, though, the first sign is spelled out as 'sh', a vowel is placed between 'sh' and 'm', and the 'w' is easier to pronounce if written as 'u', so the word comes out as 'shemu'. Wherever a letter 'u' is used, it is a 'double-u' ('w') and has the sound 'oo' as in 'boot', not 'u' as in 'but'.

For anyone hoping to study hieroglyphs in greater depth, it is recommended that they learn the way Egyptologists transliterate words, using the letters with diacritics such as š, otherwise many books on the subject will remain incomprehensible. The transliteration signs are given in the section on uniliteral signs on page 37.

How Do Hieroglyphs Work?

The hieroglyphic signs used in writing functioned in five main ways:

- as pictographs (where a word is represented by a picture)
- as ideograms (where an idea is represented by a picture)
- as phonetic symbols (where a sound is represented by a picture)
- as determinatives (used to distinguish between similar words)
- as phonetic complements (used to clarify sounds)

Many hieroglyphs had more than one function. There was no single group of hieroglyphs that operated solely as pictographs, another solely as determinatives, and so on. For example, ✶ is the sign of a star, which can act as a determinative (added to a word to show that a star or time is meant), or as an ideogram (the word 'unut', meaning 'hour'), or as a phonetic symbol (expressing the sounds 'dua' or 'seba'). When starting to learn hieroglyphs it seems impossible to know their functions, but with practice these differing functions become less confusing, and the different types of sign actually become useful aids rather than further hindrances to understanding hieroglyphs.

Pictographs

Because hieroglyphs were pictures of real things that the Egyptians saw around them, the signs could be used as pictographs (or pictograms), meaning literally 'writing with pictures'. The term 'logogram' is also used for this function of hieroglyphs and means literally 'a sign representing a word'.

This is the most simple form of writing, in which a whole word is represented by a single picture. For example, —• is a picture of an arrow and can therefore mean literally 'arrow'; ⊙ is a picture of the sun and can therefore mean 'sun'; and 🪲 is a picture of a scarab beetle and can mean literally 'scarab beetle'. Where a sign is meant to be read as a picture, it is usually accompanied by a stroke, which tells the reader that the sign is to be read only as a picture. For example, if ⌒ was supposed to be read as a picture of a mouth, it is more likely to be represented as ⌒ with | below, which is a very useful clue.

Pictographs were not a viable method of writing the complete ancient Egyptian language, because many thousands of signs would have been needed to cover the vocabulary. Also, there are severe limitations on what can be expressed in a purely pictographic form of writing. Only about 500 hieroglyphs were in common use, but over 17,000 Egyptian words are known, so although early decipherers thought that hieroglyphs formed a picture language, this was far from being the case.

Ideograms

Ideograms, literally 'idea writing', take pictographs one stage further (although some Egyptologists even classify pictographs as ideograms). The hieroglyphs are not used as the picture of a real thing, but something related to that picture. So 𓀀, an old man with a staff, can be used as the word 'iaw', meaning 'old', while 𓄋, the head of a leopard, can be used as the word 'pehti', meaning 'strength'.

Phonetic Symbols

The majority of hieroglyphs were used as phonetic symbols, also called 'sound signs', 'phonograms' or 'phonemic signs', from the Greek word *fone* meaning a sound or tone. These hieroglyphs spelled out the sounds of a word, a system that is found in languages today where alphabets are used. Even where alphabets vary dramatically, as in the English, Russian and Greek alphabets, each letter or sign represents a sound. Most alphabets have around twenty-five letters, but ancient Egyptian had a much larger number of phonetic hieroglyphs, and the system of 'sound signs' was more complicated than a true alphabet.

Hieroglyphs had three types of phonetic symbol: uniliterals, biliterals and triliterals, 'uni' being one, 'bi' two and 'tri' three. 'Literal' is from the Latin word *littera*, meaning 'letter', and so uniliteral hieroglyphs represented one sound, biliteral hieroglyphs two sounds and triliteral hieroglyphs three sounds. The full list of uniliterals is given on page 37, and examples of biliterals on page 43 and triliterals on page 50.

Vowels

When the hieroglyphs were used phonetically – as sounds – to spell out words, vowels (such as a, e, i, o, u) were rarely indicated; hieroglyphs mainly represent consonants (such as d, m, p, t). The English words 'land' and 'lend' would therefore both be written as 'lnd', while 'rover' and 'river' would both be written as 'rvr'. This is not a system peculiar to hieroglyphs, because languages such as Hebrew and Arabic commonly omit vowels in writing.

Determinatives

Determinatives (also called semograms) were hieroglyphs that determined the meaning of a word. They were not part of the spelling of a word and were not pronounced. Instead, they were added to the end of a word to give the reader some idea of its meaning. So the determinative hieroglyph , a picture of a tired man, shows that the word it accompanies means something like 'weary' or 'weak'. The sign , a picture of a circular walled settlement with a network of roads, shows that the accompanying word is a town or village (as in the place names given on page 160).

Some words in English have the same sound and spelling but a different meaning, such as 'lie' which can mean 'to lie down' or 'to tell an untruth', while 'bolt' can refer to a fastening on a door or it can be a verb meaning 'to run away'. The same is the case in ancient Egyptian. The word ⬭ ∿∿∿ 🐒 , 'rnn' (or more likely in English, 'renen'), means 'to praise', but a different determinative as in ⬭ ∿∿∿ 🦮 changes the sense: although the word is still 'renen', it now means 'to rear [a child]'.

Because there was no punctuation in hieroglyphic writing, and no spaces between words, these determinative signs are also a very good way of seeing where one word ends and another begins. Many hieroglyphic signs were only used as determinatives, so they provide useful clues about word endings and meanings. They also show that the preceding hieroglyphs were phonetic symbols, not pictographs: determinatives never come after a pictograph sign. However, although hundreds of different hieroglyphs could be used as determinatives, they were not written after every word that was spelled out with phonetic symbols.

Phonetic Complements

Also called sound complements, these were uniliteral hieroglyphs used in a special way in conjunction with biliteral and triliteral hieroglyphs. Where a scribe used a biliteral to spell out the two consonants of a single word or two consonants of a longer word, these two sounds were often spelled out yet again by uniliterals. So if the sign for 'bn' was represented by a biliteral, the letters 'b' and 'n' would also be repeated individually, sometimes in front and sometimes after. These did not act as extra letters in the word and were not pronounced (and do not need to be translated).

It became more common for only one phonetic complement to be added to a biliteral, which repeated the second, but not the first, consonant. Similarly, the last two consonants of a triliteral could be repeated by phonetic complements. For example, the biliteral ⬜ represents the two letters 'pr', but is often written with the addition of the uniliteral ⬬, the letter 'r': ⬜⬬ spells out 'pr', not 'prr'. An extra ⬬ would in fact spell out 'prr', as ⬜⬬⬬. An example of a triliteral is ▭, which represents the letters 'htp', and this could be accompanied by the phonetic complements ⌒ (the letter 't') and ▫ (the letter 'p').

Punctuation

There were no spaces between words written in hieroglyphs, no upper-case or lower-case letters (they were all the same), and no punctuation such as commas and full stops, so this sentence would be written as:

therewerenospacesbetweenwordswritteninhieroglyphsnoupper caseorlowercaseletterstheywereallthesameandnopunctuationsu chascommasandfullstopssothissentencewouldbewrittenas

Vowels were also not written, only the consonants, so in fact this sentence would appear more as:

thrwrnspcsbtwnwrdswrttnnhrglyphsnpprcsrlwrcslttrsthywrll thsmndnpncttnschscmmsndfllstpssthssntncwldbwrttns

However, hieroglyphs are not quite as awkward to understand as this sentence, because the hieroglyphs of each word were grouped together (see page 56).

Uniliterals

As explained under 'How Do Hieroglyphs Work?' on page 28, hieroglyphs representing a single consonant or sound are called uniliterals (they can also be called uniconsonantals). There were around twenty-five of these, with some variants, all technically consonants (such as b, g, t), although some are 'weak' consonants and resemble vowels in the way they need to be written in an English alphabet. These uniliteral signs are really equivalent to an alphabet, although the Egyptians had no concept of an alphabet and had no special names for these signs. In a language such as English, only the alphabet is used to spell words, but uniliteral hieroglyphs were mixed with other types of hieroglyph to spell out words. Examples of uniliterals include ∼∼∼, which depicted rippling water, but was actually used to write the sound 'n', and ⌋, which depicted a foot and lower leg, but was used to write the sound 'b'.

These uniliteral signs were the most commonly used hieroglyphs and need to be learned by anyone starting out in hieroglyphs. The Egyptians found these signs particularly useful when it came to spelling out the sounds of foreign names that they encountered later in their history, names such as Ptolemy, Cleopatra and Alexander.

There are special signs that Egyptologists use for transliterating (see page 25) these hieroglyphs (that is, for converting them into a modern-day script). In the list below, the uniliteral hieroglyphs are in the order they are given in dictionaries of hieroglyphs. The order does not follow the European alphabet (a, b, c, d and so on). Instead, it is more like a, i, y, another (different-sounding) a, u, b and so on! The next column gives the transliteration sign used by Egyptologists, and the third column gives the name of the transliteration sign (such as 'aleph', 'm', 'fourth h'). The fourth column gives the more simplified transliteration used in this book. The final column describes the actual hieroglyph (such as a vulture), its possible pronunciation, where clarification is needed, and its Gardiner number. The Gardiner numbers refer to the classification used by most Egyptologists, explained under 'What Are Hieroglyphs?' on page 13.

Uniliteral Hieroglyph	Transliteration		Letters used in this book	What the signs were (Gardiner numbers at the end in brackets)
	Sign	Name		
ꜣ	*ꜣ*	aleph	a, or ah	An Egyptian vulture (*Neophron percnopterus*). The sound it originally represented is uncertain, possibly something called a glottal stop, a sound that was made in the larynx (as in Cockney 'bottle' when the two 't's are pronounced at the back of the throat, giving 'bo'l'). In this book 'a' or 'ah' is used for this sign (pronounced 'a' as in the English word 'part' or the German word *Vater*). It is technically a weak consonant, not a vowel (G1)
	i, j or *i*	yodh	i, or y	A flowering reed, the letter 'i' or 'y', was technically a weak consonant and not a vowel. It was possibly not even pronounced very often. It perhaps sounded more like a 'y' in the English 'yes' or the German *ja* (M17)
(or \\)	*y, ii*	y	y	Two flowering reeds represented a much stronger sound of 'y' than the hieroglyph above (M17 and Z4)

Uniliteral Hieroglyph	Transliteration Sign	Name	Letters used in this book	What the signs were (Gardiner numbers at the end in brackets)
▃◻	ꜥ	ayin	a	A person's arm represented a guttural sound, made deep in the throat, which occurs in Arabic and Hebrew. It is usually expressed in English as an 'a' (D36)
🐦 (or ℓ)	*w*	w	u, or w	A quail chick formed the sound 'oo', 'u' or even 'w' as in the English words 'boot' or 'wind'. Hieratic writing later used the sign ℓ instead, which was in turn used as a hieroglyphic sign (G43 and Z7)
⅃	*b*	b	b	A lower leg and foot of a person (D58)
◻	*p*	p	p	A reed matting stool (one of the commonest items of furniture) (Q3)
⌐	*f*	f	f	A viper with two horns (I9)
🦉 (or ⬡)	*m*	m	m	An owl (the only bird shown in a hieroglyph full-face, and not sideways). A sign of unknown origin (⬡) was an alternative (G17 and Aa13)

Uniliteral Hieroglyph	Transliteration Sign	Name	Letters used in this book	What the signs were (Gardiner numbers at the end in brackets)
〰〰 (or 𓋹)	*n*	n	n	A sign for rippling water, or water with waves. The Red Crown was a later alternative sign for 'n' (N35 and S3)
⬯	*r*	r	r	An outline of a person's mouth (D21)
⬚	*h*	h	h	A plan view of a reed shelter or hut was used for the letter 'h', as in the English word 'hill' (O4)
𓎛	*ḥ*	dotted h	h	A twisted wick (probably made of cloth soaked in fat) used in a lamp represented a hard, emphatic 'h' (V28)
⊜	*ḫ*	third h	ch, or kh	A circular sign with horizontal lines, an uncertain sign but thought possibly to be a human placenta, represented the sound 'ch' or 'kh' (as in the German *Buch* or the Scottish 'loch') (Aa1)
⊶	*ẖ*	fourth h	ch	A plan view of an animal's belly and udder. It possibly represented the sound 'ch', as in the German *ich* (F32)

Uniliteral Hieroglyph	Transliteration Sign	Name	Letters used in this book	What the signs were (Gardiner numbers at the end in brackets)
—◦—	z	z	s, or z	A doorbolt, the type used to close double doors from the outside (as in a temple) (O34)
⎮	s	s	s	A folded length of woven cloth (usually termed 'bolt of cloth', which can cause confusion with the doorbolt above) (S29)
⬓	š	shin	sh	A plan view of an artificial pool or basin (N37)
△	q, or ḳ	q	q, or k	A sideways view of a sandy hill-slope was an emphatic 'k' or 'q', as in the English word 'queen' (N29)
⌔	k	k	k	A basket with a handle (V31)
▨	g	g	g	The side view of a circular stand for a jar. It represented a hard 'g', as in the word 'gold' (W11)
⌒	t	t	t	A side view of a loaf of bread (X1)
⬡	ṯ	second t	tj, or tsh	A hobble tethering rope for animals (V13)
⬭	d	d	d	A hand of a person (D46)

Uniliteral Hieroglyph	Transliteration Sign	Name	Letters used in this book	What the signs were (Gardiner numbers at the end in brackets)
	ḏ	second d	j, or dj	A cobra at rest was the sign for the sound 'j' or 'dj' (as in the English word 'joke') (I10)

Biliterals

Biliterals (also called biconsonantals) are double consonants. They are individual hieroglyphs that represent two sounds in the same sign – not vowels like 'i' and 'e', but consonants like 'g' and 't'. The biliteral sign ⊂⊃ is a picture of a gaming board (viewed from the side, with the gaming pieces on top), and represented a combination of the two letters 'mn' (instead of using 🦉 and 〰). Similarly, ⟨ is a picture of a hoe, and represented the two letters 'mr' combined (instead of using 🦉 and ⊂◯). These biliterals numbered over eighty, and examples are given below. Because the universal transliteration alphabet has not been used here (see page 26), it may look as if some of these hieroglyphs have vowels and even more than two consonants. For example, the hieroglyph ∿◻ would be transliterated as $\underline{h}w$ in the universal transliteration alphabet, but it is easier to pronounce if it is written as 'khu'.

Where hieroglyphs represent sounds such as 'mt', 'nh' and 'wr', the vowel 'e' can also be introduced to make them easier to pronounce ('met', 'neh' and 'wer'). Some hieroglyphs had more than one sound or function, so the ones given below may not always operate as biliterals. For example, the hieroglyph ⟩ can be a biliteral 'hb' and a triliteral 'shna'.

The Gardiner numbers refer to the classification used by most Egyptologists, explained under 'What Are Hieroglyphs?' on page 13.

Biliteral Hieroglyph	Letters used in this book	What the Hieroglyph Depicts (Gardiner number in brackets)
	ir	Eye (D4)
	ka	Two arms raised (D28)
	chn	Two arms rowing with an oar (D33)
	khu	An arm holding a flail (D43)
	mt	Penis (D52)
	ib	Kid (E8)
	iw	Newborn calf (E9)
	ru	Recumbent lion (E23)
	un	Hare (E34)
	up	Ox horns (F13)
	ph	Rear of lion (F22)

Biliteral Hieroglyph	Letters used in this book	What the Hieroglyph Depicts (Gardiner number in brackets)
	shd	Water skin (F30)
	ms	Three fox skins tied together (F31)
	ib	Heart (F34)
	aw	Spine with spinal cord at each end (F40)
	mt	Vulture (G14)
	nh	Guinea fowl (G21)
	akh	Crested ibis (G25)
	gm	Black ibis (G28)
	ba	Jabiru (G29)
	ak	Cormorant (G35)
	ur	Swallow (G36)
	gb	White-fronted goose (G38)
	sa	Pintail duck (G39)

Biliteral Hieroglyph	Letters used in this book	What the Hieroglyph Depicts (Gardiner number in brackets)
	pa	Pintail duck flying (G40)
	pa	Pintail duck landing (G41)
	ja	Duckling (G47)
	shu	Feather (H6)
	km	Crocodile scales (I6)
	cha	Oxyrhynchus fish (K4)
	kht	Tree branch with twigs (M3)
	sha	Pool with flowers (M8)
	kha	Lotus lily (M12)
	ha	Clump of papyrus (M16)
	su	Sedge plant (M23)
	is	Bundle of reeds (M40)
	ta	Strip of flat land with sand (N16)

Biliteral Hieroglyph	Letters used in this book	What the Hieroglyph Depicts (Gardiner number in brackets)
⌒	kha	Sunrise over mountain (N28)
〰	mu	Water with ripples or waves (N35a)
⊏⊐	mr	Canal (N36)
⊏⊐	pr	Plan of house (O1)
𓊽	aa	Wooden column (O29)
◉	sp	Threshing floor with grain (O50)
𓊽	djd	Reed column (R11)
𓌉	hdj	Stone mace (T3)
⇓	sn	Arrowhead (T22)
⋀	chr	Butcher's block (T28)
⌇	nm	Butcher's knife (T34)
⌐	ma	Sickle (U1)
⌐	mr	Hoe (U6)

Biliteral Hieroglyph	Letters used in this book	What the Hieroglyph Depicts (Gardiner number in brackets)
⌄	hb	Plough (U13)
⊨	tm	Sledge (U15)
⌇	ab, mr	Chisel (U23)
⌓	dja	Fire drill (U29)
⌷	ta	Kiln (U30)
⌇	ti	Pestle (U33)
⌇	hm	Launderer's club (U36)
⌓	wa	Lasso (V4)
⌾	shs	Looped cord (V6)
⌾	shn	Looped cord (V7)
⧻	sa	Cattle hobble (V16)
⌇	wdj	Cord wound on a stick (V24)
⊂⊃	adj	Weaver's shuttle (V26)

Biliteral Hieroglyph	Letters used in this book	What the Hieroglyph Depicts (Gardiner number in brackets)
	sk	Fibre swab (V29)
	nb	Basket (V31)
	hs	Ceramic water jar (W14)
	mi	Milk jug with carrying net (W19)
	nu	Ceramic pot (W24)
	mn	Gaming board (Y5)

Triliterals

Triliterals, also called triconsonantals, are triple consonants. They are individual hieroglyphs that represent three sounds in the same sign – not vowels like 'a' and 'o', but consonants like 'k' and 'p'. There were around seventy triliterals, most of which actually spelled out a single word, such as ⌐, which was a picture of a flag on a pole (an emblem of divinity), but which represented the sounds 'ntr' (rather than using the signs ⌇⌐⌐) and spelled out the word for 'god'. The sign ⌐, which is a picture of an adze on a block of wood, expressed the three sounds of 'stp' combined, rather than using the three signs ⌐⌐⌐. Several examples of triliterals are given below, but because the universal transliteration alphabet has not been used here (see page 26), it may look as if some of these hieroglyphs have vowels and even more than three consonants. For example, the hieroglyph 𓆣 should be transliterated as *ḫpr*, but it is easier to pronounce when written as 'khpr' (or with added vowels as 'kheper').

Where hieroglyphs represent sounds such as 'ntr' and 'spd', the vowel 'e' can be introduced to make them easier to pronounce ('neter', 'seped'). Some hieroglyphs had more than one sound or function, so the ones given below may not always operate in this way. For example, the hieroglyph 𓊃 can be a biliteral 'sk' and a triliteral 'wah'.

The Gardiner numbers refer to the classification used by most Egyptologists, explained under 'What Are Hieroglyphs?' on page 13.

Triliteral Hieroglyph	Letters Used In This Book	What the Hieroglyph Depicts (Gardiner number in brackets)
	khnt	Person's eye, nose, cheek (D19)
	wsr	Head and neck of jackal (F12)
	idn, sdjm	Ear of an ox (F21)
	whm	Leg and hoof of ox (F25)
	sab	Cow skin (with tail) (F28)
	nfr	Animal heart and windpipe (F35)
	sma	Animal lungs and windpipe (F36)
	isu	Joint of meat (F44)
	mut	Vulture (G14)
	asha	Lizard (I1)

Triliteral Hieroglyph	Letters Used In This Book	What the Hieroglyph Depicts (Gardiner number in brackets)
	khpr	Scarab beetle (L1)
	ima	Tree (M1)
	wadj	Papyrus plant (M13)
	nkhb	Rush plant (M22)
	shma	Flowering sedge (M26)
	spd	Thorn (M44)
	wbn	Sun with rays (N8)
	sba, dua	Star (N14)
	shsp	Fence (O42)
	uha	Boat with net (P4)
	aha	Boat's mast (P6)
	khrw	Oar (P8)
	htp	Loaf on a mat (R4)

Triliteral Hieroglyph	Letters Used In This Book	What the Hieroglyph Depicts (Gardiner number in brackets)
⸮	ntr	Flag on pole (R8)
⸮	mdjh	Band of cloth (S10)
▭	sia	Cloth with fringe (S32)
⸮	ankh	Sandal strap (S34)
⸮	hka	Crook (S38)
⸮	aut	Shepherd's crook (S39)
⸮	was	Animal-headed staff or sceptre (S40)
⸮	djam	Animal-headed staff or sceptre with spiral shaft (S41)
⸮	aba	Sceptre (S42)
⸮	swn	Arrow (T11)
⸮	rudj, rud	Bowstring (T12)
⸮	sshm	Knife sharpener (T31)

Triliteral Hieroglyph	Letters Used In This Book	What the Hieroglyph Depicts (Gardiner number in brackets)
	shna	Plough (U13)
	stp	Adze on a block of wood (U21)
	uba	Drill for cutting beads (U26)
	khsf	Spindle (U34)
	shsr	Looped cord (V6)
	wah	Fibre swab (V29)
	chnm	Stone jug with handle (W9)
	hnw	Cup (W10)
	khnt	Rack of ceramic water jars (W17)
	sua	Crossed sticks (Z9)
	maa	Pedestal or platform (Aa11)

The Way To Read Hieroglyphs

English is written and read horizontally from left to right, while Arabic is written and read horizontally from right to left. Hieroglyphs could be written and read horizontally in two directions: either from left to right or from right to left, although the top line was always read first, then the line beneath, and so on. In hieroglyphic inscriptions written in vertical columns, the hieroglyphs were read from top to bottom (never bottom to top), either starting with the left-hand or the right-hand column. The direction of writing and reading in both horizontal lines and vertical columns of hieroglyphs depended on the direction in which the hieroglyphs faced.

Because of this variation and flexibility, scribes could compose their writing artistically, particularly when it accompanied other pictures, such as those of people and gods in tomb paintings. The writing would often face the same way as a person or god being depicted, so if two people sat opposite each other, the writing would be divided in the same painting into two groups facing two different ways.

The method of deciding which way hieroglyphs should be read is to work out the direction in which they are facing. For some hieroglyphs, it is easy to see which way they face. For example, the hieroglyphs 🜚 (an old man with a stick), 🜚 (a woman giving birth) and 🜚 (a giraffe) all face left here, while 🜚 (a heron), 🜚 (a man worshipping) and 🜚 (a king with the Red Crown) all face right here. For many hieroglyphs it is impossible to work out which way they are facing, such as ⋀ (a thorn), ◠ (a mountain range) and ⋂ (an obelisk), but this is rarely a problem, since the direction of only one hieroglyph needs to be identified to know which way a line of hieroglyphs should be read.

The way to read the hieroglyphs is to look into the faces or the front of the signs being depicted, not at the back of them. If a queue of people is imagined, all facing the same way, then the first one in the queue is read first. For example, the word for 'shield' is 🜚🜚🜚🜚 ('ikem'). The direction of reading is best taken from 🜚, an owl, who is here facing left (although its head is turned to face the reader). With increased familiarity with the hieroglyphs, it will also be apparent that the other signs are also facing left: ⸡, the reed sign for the letter 'i'; and ◁, which depicts crocodile scales and stands for 'km'; and the last sign 🜚 meaning 'cowskin', from which the shield would have been made. Because of the direction of the signs, this word is read from left to right.

The same word 🜚🜚◁⸡ is read from right to left, because the signs are now facing right, while they can also appear as:

 when they are read from top to bottom. Because they are facing left, the reader would start with this column and would then read the next column to the right.

In the word 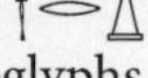 ('mer'), meaning 'pyramid', the direction of the three hieroglyphs cannot be worked out, but the word is not likely to occur on its own, so the direction of reading can be worked out from adjacent words.

Linear hieroglyphs (see page 8) were usually written in columns, with the signs facing right. The signs in an individual column would be read starting at the top and working down to the bottom. The individual columns were read from right to left.

Hieratic (see page 8) was at first written in either horizontal rows or vertical columns, like hieroglyphs, but from about 1800 BC it was mainly written in horizontal rows, with vertical columns reserved for religious texts. This handwriting form of hieroglyphs was only written from right to left, with the signs facing right. Like hieratic, demotic was written in horizontal lines, from right to left. The later development of Coptic was also written in horizontal lines, but from left to right, following ancient Greek on which the script was based.

Most hieroglyphs were not written in an exact horizontal line or vertical column, but were arranged in groups, with tall signs standing on their own and smaller signs positioned one above the other. This can make it difficult at first to work out which hieroglyph should be read first, as in the word . This word spells 'mnmnt' (which is easier to pronounce as 'menmenet') and means 'a herd' (of cattle). The hieroglyphs should actually be read in the following order 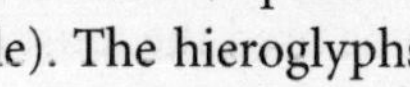.

Pronunciation

Ancient Egyptian is a dead language. The written language survives, but nobody can be certain how the language was spoken. The main clues come from Coptic, which was a very late version of ancient Egyptian (see page 6), because it is known how the latest version of Coptic was spoken. Clues can also be gained from how the Egyptians wrote the words of foreign languages (as in the ancient Greek names of rulers such as Ptolemy and Cleopatra). A few more clues can be gained from how other ancient languages wrote down Egyptian words. There were probably various ways to speak ancient Egyptian, with different dialects in different regions and with the language changing over the hundreds of years that it was spoken.

A major difficulty arises for anyone learning hieroglyphs, because the Egyptians did not write vowels, so we are faced with words without vowels like 'mnmn', 's', 'pr' or 'ndb', with no idea how to pronounce them. For convenience, a vowel can be placed between some letters to make the words easier to learn and to pronounce. The vowel that tends to be used the most in English is an 'e', and so this is commonly placed between the consonants of ancient Egyptian words. Other vowels are sometimes used, though, mainly to make the sound of the words less monotonous. The words 'mnmn', 's', 'pr', 'ndb' might therefore be written today as 'menmen', 'se', 'per' and 'nedeb'.

Your Name

Because hieroglyphs look so very different from most, if not all, other types of writing, it can be fascinating to write your own name and those of your family and friends in hieroglyphs. When the Egyptians found it necessary to write down the names of foreigners (such as the Greek rulers Alexander the Great and Ptolemy), they mainly used uniliteral signs (see page 37) with some biliterals (see page 43). This is by far the most straightforward way of writing your own name and it is a way of putting into practice some of the signs seen in the previous pages.

This is not a scientific exercise and there is no single correct way of writing non-Egyptian words in hieroglyphs. When writing English words in hieroglyphs, the following translations of English sounds into hieroglyphs are the ones most commonly used. This is not an Egyptian alphabet, but merely a guide to writing your name today. There is no difference in hieroglyphs between upper-case letters (A, B) and lower-case letters (a, b).

English Alphabet	Hieroglyphs You Can Use
a	𓄿, possibly ◡▭
b	𓃀
c	For a hard 'c', as in Carol, use ◠; for a soft 'c', as in Celia, use ❘
ch	For a 'ch' sound, as in Charles, use ▱; for a hard 'ch', as in Michael, use ◠ or alternatively ◉ or ◉
d	◠
e	This was not written, but you can use ❪
f	◠
g	For a hard 'g' as in Gail use ▣; for a soft 'g', as in George, use ❰
h	For a hard 'h', as in Harry, use ❁; for a soft or silent 'h', as in John, use ▢
i	❪
j	❰
k	◠; for a hard 'ch', as in Christine, alternatives to 'k' are ◉ and ◉
l	⌂. This is a biliteral sign, used for the sound 'ru'. There was no 'l' sound, but the Egyptians did use this sign for 'l' in the Greek name Ptolemy
m	𓄿, or ▱

English Alphabet	Hieroglyphs You Can Use
n	~~~~ , or [glyph]
o	[glyph]. This is a biliteral sign, used for the sound 'ooa' or 'ua', but also used by the Egyptians for the 'o' in the Greek name Ptolemy
p	[glyph]
ph	For an 'f'-sounding 'ph', as in Christopher, use [glyph]
q	[glyph]
r	[glyph]
s	[glyph]
sh	for a 'sh' sound, as in Charlotte or Joshua, use [glyph]
t	[glyph]
u	[glyph], or [glyph]
v	You will need to use the 'b' sound [glyph]
w	[glyph], or [glyph]
x	This sound is best spelled out as 'ks' using the two hieroglyphs [glyph] [glyph]
y	[glyph], or \\
z	[glyph]

If a name does not look right in hieroglyphs, alternatives can be tried, because often there is more than one way of spelling it. For example, the name 'Sophie' can be written by changing every letter into a hieroglyph. This produces ⸢𓊪𓆓𓏏𓏭𓏭⸣ , but the sounds of the name ('sofi') can also be changed into hieroglyphs to produce ⸢𓊪𓆓𓏭⸣ . The ancient Egyptians tended to change the sounds of the name into hieroglyphs, but nowadays the letter-by-letter spelling of a name is more often used.

Other hieroglyphs (determinatives) can be added to names, such as the hieroglyph ⸢𓀀⸣ in ⸢𓂋𓃀𓂋𓏏⸣ (Robert), which shows it is the name of a boy or a man. The extra hieroglyphs ⸢𓁐⸣ in the name ⸢𓎡𓃭𓂋⸣ (Clare) show that this is the name of a girl or a woman.

Names can be made more important by putting them inside 'cartouches' such as: (𓄿𓃭𓃭𓀀) (Ella), because the ancient Egyptians used cartouches for the names of royalty (see page 95), as in (𓄿𓃭𓇋𓊪𓄿𓂧𓂋𓄿) (Queen Cleopatra).

Here are some names written in hieroglyphs, but any other name can be written by using the alphabet given above:

Adrian	𓄿𓂧𓂋𓇋𓄿𓈖
Alan	𓄿𓃭𓄿𓈖
Alexander	𓄿𓃭𓇋𓎡𓄿𓈖𓂧𓂋
Alexandra	𓄿𓃭𓇋𓎡𓄿𓈖𓂧𓂋𓄿

Alice

Alison

Amanda

Amy

Andrew

Ann

Anne

Anthony

Antony

Benjamin

Brian

Caroline

Charles

Charlotte

Chloe

Christine

Christopher

Claire

Clare

Name	Hieroglyphs
Craig	
Daniel	
Darren	
David	
Deborah	
Derek	
Diana	
Diane	
Douglas	
Edward	
Elizabeth	
Ella	
Emily	
Emma	
Frances	
Francis	
Gail	
George	
Gillian	

Gordon	
Graham	
Guy	
Hannah	
Harry	
Helen	
Iain	
Ian	
Jack	
Jacqueline	
James	
Jane	
Jean	
Jennifer	
Jeremy	
Jessica	
Jill	
Joanne	
John	

Name	Hieroglyphs
Jonathan	
Joseph	
Joshua	
Judith	
Julian	
Julie	
Justin	
Karen	
Katherine	
Kelly	
Kenneth	
Kerry	
Kevin	
Laura	
Lawrence	
Leanne	
Lesley	
Linda	
Lisa	

Louise

Lucy

Luke

Madeleine

Malcolm

Margaret

Marion

Mark

Martin

Mary

Matthew

Maureen

Megan

Michael

Miriam

Muriel

Natalie

Nathan

Neil

Name	Hieroglyphs
Nicholas	
Nicola	
Nigel	
Oliver	
Owen	
Pamela	
Patrick	
Paul	
Peter	
Philip	
Philippa	
Poppy	
Rachel	
Ralph	
Rebecca	
Richard	
Robert	
Robin	
Roger	

Rosemary

Rowena

Roy

Russell

Ruth

Ryan

Samantha

Samuel

Sandra

Sara

Sarah

Sebastian

Sheila

Simon

Sophie

Stephen

Steven

Stuart

Susan

Suzanne	
Thomas	
Timothy	
Tracy	
Trevor	
Valerie	
Victoria	
William	
Zoe	

Plurals

In English, the most common way to make a plural is to add an 's' to a noun, so that 'house' becomes 'houses'. The Egyptians expressed a plural by giving their nouns a 'w' ending (or 'wt' for feminine nouns), using the hieroglyph 𓅱, which is the uniliteral sign for 'w' or 'u'. They also included three strokes, either 𓏪 or 𓏥, or more rarely three dots ooo. This plural did not refer to three, but to any number.

The word for a wife or woman is 𓈞𓏏𓁐, 'hmt', but the plural in full would be 𓈞𓅱𓏏𓁐𓏥 ('wives'). The 'w' hieroglyph is technically at the end of the word, because the other two signs were additions: the female indicator 𓏏 (see page 62) and a determinative 𓁐 (see page 31). In reality, 𓅱 ('w') was rarely written for plurals because it was a weak consonant, and the plural form that was used instead was 𓈞𓏏𓁐𓏪, 'hmwt'. In transliteration, the 'w' is written in order to indicate the plural, even if it was not specifically written in the hieroglyphs, and the female indicator 't' is written after the plural 'w'. In order to make it easier to pronounce this word, it could be written as 'hemut'.

The oldest method of writing a plural was to repeat a sign three times, so 𓂋𓈖, 'rn' meaning 'mouth', becomes in the plural form

⟨glyph⟩, 'rnw'. (These words are easier to pronounce if spelled as 'ren' and 'renu'). In time, this system became archaic and was replaced by three strokes. For ⟨glyph⟩, 'per', meaning 'house', the plural ('peru') was initially ⟨glyph⟩, and then ⟨glyph⟩ or ⟨glyph⟩.

The Egyptians also had several ways of showing a pair of things, which is plural of two things only (a dual), with words ending in ⟨glyph⟩ 'ty' for feminine words and ⟨glyph⟩ or ⟨glyph⟩ 'wy' for masculine words (although these hieroglyphs were not always shown in full). One way of indicating two things was simply to write the word twice, so that ⟨glyph⟩, 'ntr', a god, is written ⟨glyph⟩ for two gods ('ntrwy').

Determinatives (see page 31) were also doubled when expressing two things. One sister would be ⟨glyph⟩, 'sent', while two sisters was ⟨glyph⟩, 'senty'. One brother would be ⟨glyph⟩, 'sen', while two brothers is ⟨glyph⟩, 'senwy'.

Numbers

Hieroglyphic numbers are probably the easiest of the hieroglyphs to understand. The Egyptians used a decimal system of counting, with ones, tens and hundreds. In English, ten numerals (from 0 to 9) are used, but in Egyptian six basic numerals were used to cover single units, tens, hundreds, thousands, ten thousands, and hundred thousands. There was no sign for zero.

Except for one ('wa', ⌐), numbers were usually written with symbols (as in 3, 27), not in words (as in three, twenty-seven). Most of the Egyptian names for the numbers are unknown, but have been reconstructed from the later Coptic language (see page 6).

The basic six numbers were:

| ('wa'): 1
∩ ('medju'): 10
𐤏 ('shet'): 100
𓏺 ('kha'): 1,000
𓆼 ('djeba'): 10,000
𓆐 ('hefen'): 100,000

The sign for 1,000 is the lotus lily plant, that for 10,000 is a finger, and that for 100,000 a tadpole.

Any number could be constructed by combining and/or repeating one or more of these basic six numbers. A hieroglyphic number is read by simply adding up what the signs represent. For example, ℓ||||| is ℓ (100) plus ||||| (5), totalling 105. The higher numerals always come first, so if the writing was being done from left to right, it would appear as in the following examples:

|||| 4

∩||||| 14

ℓℓℓ??   301

𝄿𝄿𝄿𝄿𝄿   50,000

⌇⌇ ℓℓℓℓ??∩∩∩|| 2,432

If the writing was done from right to left, then 2,432 would appear as ||∩∩∩????ℓℓℓℓ⌇⌇.

There was also a sign for one million 𝍱 ('heh'), although this tended to be used more to imply 'many' or 'too many to count', rather than the precise figure.

Fractions are not commonly found, but they were generally expressed by placing ⌒ (the letter 'r') above the numeral. The fraction for ⅕ (which has a numerator of 1 and a denominator of 5) would be ⌒|||. For fractions with numerators larger than 1 (such as ⅖, ⅘), the Egyptians combined several fractions, not necessarily with the same denominator. A simple example is ⌒||| ⌒|||, which equals ⅖.

A Little More Grammar

Some elements of the grammar of the ancient Egyptian language, such as plurals, have already been mentioned, but anyone intending to make a serious study of hieroglyphs should learn all the elements of the grammar – too large a topic to be covered in detail here. However, some aspects of grammar can help immensely, and a few further examples are set out below.

Egyptian sentences do not always have verbs, but they need a verb to be translated into English. For example, the two words 'man old' would be translated in English as 'the man is old'. Verbs in English have various forms (such as 'writes', 'wrote', 'writing', 'written'), and verbs are equally complex in Egyptian, forming the most extensive part of any book on Egyptian grammar.

In a language such as English, a few nouns and associated words are obviously female (such as 'mother', 'she', 'her'), some are masculine (such as 'brother', 'he', 'his'), while the majority are technically neuter (such as 'tree', 'pot', 'river', 'it', 'its'). Adjectives remain the same in English, whatever their use, such as 'a good book' or 'a good daughter'. In a language such as French, all nouns are either feminine or masculine, singular or plural, and adjectives reflect the gender and number of the nouns. For example *un livre intéressant* ('an interesting book' – masculine, singular) but *des lettres intéres-santes* ('interesting letters' – feminine, plural). Often in French, a 'masculine-sounding' word will be feminine, and vice versa, such as *la guerre* ('war' – feminine) and *le sein* ('breast' – masculine).

In Egyptian, there are two genders – masculine and feminine – and so all nouns have to be one or the other, even if they do not always seem masculine or feminine in nature. Most feminine nouns have a 't', ⌒, added to the end of a word (but placed before any determinatives), although there are also a few masculine nouns which end in a 't'. The word for 'house', ⌷, is masculine, but the word for 'town', ⊛, is feminine and has a female 't' ending.

The word for 'man' ('s', perhaps pronounced as 'se') is ⌐🏃, with ⌐ being the letter 's' and 🏃 being the determinative for a man. The word for 'woman' is 🧎: the determinative has changed to a female one, and a letter 't', ⌒, has also been added, so the noun now reads as 'st' (or 'set').

Adjectives (such as 'good', 'large') change their endings accord-ing to the noun they are accompanying, as happens in languages such as French and Latin. So a 'good man' is ⌐🏃🍶 and a 'good woman' is 🧎🍶. If the masculine noun is plural, the adjective would also be shown in the plural (for example, with ⎮), but the plural is rarely shown in feminine adjectives.

There was no exactly equivalent word for 'of' (the genitive), but in Middle Egyptian the 'possessing noun' (the one that owned something, or the one to which something belonged) came second. The phrase 'the scribe of the temple' would be written 'scribe temple'. The exception to the rule was when the possessing noun was the word 'god', 'king' or something associated such as the name of a god, as these would be placed first out of respect, as in many of the pharaohs' names (see page 95). This is called 'honorific transposition'.

An alternative method to show possession was to link the two words: if the first noun (not the possessing noun) was masculine and singular, then the uniliteral ᠆᠆᠆ ('n', more easily pronounced as 'en') was used as a link; if the first noun was masculine and a dual or a plural, then ʘı ('nw' or 'nu') was used as a link; but if the first noun was feminine, either singular or plural, then ᨓ was used.

In Middle Egyptian there were no definite or indefinite articles, so the word for 'a pen' would be the same as 'the pen'. In Late Egyptian (which was not written in hieroglyphs – see page 7), words for 'the' and 'a' do occur in the written language.

There was also no word for conjunctions such as 'and' and 'or'; one noun usually follows another, so that 'river and desert' would be 'river desert'.

There were words for different pronouns (words that stand for nouns such as 'he', 'him', 'my', 'that'). Some were added to the ends of nouns (as suffixes), so 'a house' or 'the house' is ⬒, while 'his house' is ⬒, 'prf' or 'peref'. ᨓ is a singular masculine suffix pronoun that can be used for 'he', 'his' or 'him'. It was always added to the end of a word, and Egyptologists often transliterate it with a dot (as '.f'), so 'prf' would be written as 'pr.f'. The same ending occurs in 'his houses' (plural) as ⬒, while 'their house' would be ⬒, 'pr.sn' or 'persen'. 𓈖𓏤𓏼𓏼 is the plural suffix pronoun for 'they' or 'their'.

There were also numerous prepositions, such as 𓇋𓈖 ('in'), meaning 'by'; 𓅓 ('em'), meaning 'in'; 𓏠𓏭 ('mi'), meaning 'like'; and 𓈖 ('en'), meaning 'to' or 'for'.

Hieroglyphs In Action

A Few Examples

When faced with individual words in a hieroglyphic text, it is necessary to try to assess the different function and meaning of the various hieroglyphs. The following examples will give some clues as to what to expect:

𓏤𓃀𓅿★ is the word for 'sba' (or 'seba'), meaning 'star'. 𓏤 can be an abbreviation for 'seneb' in 𓋴𓏤𓏤 (see page 165), but otherwise it is most likely to be the uniliteral hieroglyph for 's'. 𓃀 can on its own read 'bu', meaning 'place' or 'position', but in that case it would tend to be written as 𓃀𓏤. It is more likely to be the uniliteral hieroglyph for 'b'. Although 𓅿 can mean simply 'a bird', it is nearly always used as the uniliteral hieroglyph for 'a'. So far this word spells 'sba' (or 'seba'), a word that can mean 'star'. The final hieroglyph is the sign for a star, and so it is being used as a determinative, indicating that this word does indeed mean 'star'.

𓏠𓏠𓃒 is the word for mnmnt (or menmenet), meaning 'a herd'. This consists of the biliteral hieroglyph 𓏠 for 'mn' and the uniliteral hieroglyph 𓈖 for 'n'. The two instances of 𓈖 are acting as phonetic complements (see page 32), emphasising the 'n' in 'mn'.

79

The hieroglyph ⌒ is a 't', showing that this is a feminine noun (see page 76), while the hieroglyph of the cow is a determinative, showing that the word is associated with cattle. The three strokes beneath the cow is a plural sign, showing that this is a plural in the sense that several cattle would make up a herd; the word does not mean several herds, so it is a 'false plural' word.

𒀭 is the word for 'shsr' (or 'sheser'), meaning 'arrow'. The hieroglyph ᚼ can be a biliteral for 'shs' or (as here) a triliteral for 'shsr'. The next two hieroglyphs ᛁ and ⌒ give the clue that ᚼ is 'shsr', because they are phonetic complements emphasising the 's' and 'r' letters. The final hieroglyph is of an arrow and is a determinative, showing that the word means 'an arrow' or something associated with an arrow.

𓏃 is the word for 'snwy' (or 'senwy'), meaning 'two brothers'. The hieroglyph ᛁ is of an arrowhead and is a biliteral for 'sn'. The next hieroglyph ∼∼∼ is the letter 'n', acting as a phonetic complement to emphasise the 'n' in 'sn'. The hieroglyph 𓏲 is the uniliteral for the letter 'w', representing a plural, and ⑊, the uniliteral for 'y', expresses the dual plural (that is, two brothers only). The final two hieroglyphs both represent a seated man, the determinative for a man, showing that the word is something to do with a man; two seated men are shown because of the dual plural.

Time Chart

Before moving on to see how hieroglyphs operated within the names of pharaohs, the following dates give a checklist of what was happening at any one time in Egypt. Most of the dates refer to the reigns of the pharaohs. Pharaohs were the kings of Egypt, mostly men, very occasionally women. The word 'pharaoh' is commonly used instead of 'king', because this was a term used by the ancient Greeks when translating the Egyptian hieroglyphs (*per-aa*), which originally meant a great house or palace and was then used for the king himself.

In the third century BC an Egyptian high priest by the name of Manetho wrote down in ancient Greek a list of the rulers of Egypt, dividing them into thirty dynasties or groups. This flawed system is still used today, with the addition of dynasty 0 for early rulers, although there remains a big problem concerning dates. Dates for ancient Egypt are notoriously inaccurate, constantly disputed and vary from book to book. Up to around 650 BC, dates can be very uncertain and are a constant source of argument. The dates when Pepi I ruled, for example, are given as 2343–2297 BC in one book, 2289–2255 BC in another, and different again in other books. New research and new discoveries are constantly changing ideas on dating. The dates for the pharaohs given here follow those in Ian Shaw and Paul Nicholson (1995), *British Museum Dictionary of Ancient Egypt*.

Some dates overlap, because different pharaohs could rule different parts of Egypt at the same time, as in dynasties 7 to 11. Other overlapping dates occur when a pharaoh's successor (often his son) shared power (a co-regency), as in the case of Senusret I who shared power with his father Amenemhet I for up to a decade before his father's death. With new ideas on dates, some dynasties appear in a confused order: for example, dynasty 25 begins before dynasty 24. All dates are BC ('before Christ'), and so they work in an opposite way to the dates of the last 2,000 years. A date of 2000 BC, for example, occurred 500 years before a date of 1500 BC.

Earliest hieroglyphs	3500
Early Dynastic Period	
Dynasty 0 begins	3150
Scorpion	3150
Narmer	3100
Dynasty 1 begins	3100
Aha	3100
Djer	3000
Djet	2980

Den	2950
Anedjib	2925
Semerkhet	2900
Qaa	2890
Dynasty 2 begins	2890
Hetepsekhemwy	2890
Raneb	2865
Nynetjer	?
Peribsen	2700
Khasekhemwy	2686

Old Kingdom

Dynasty 3 begins	2686
Sanakht	2686–2667
Djoser	2667–2648
Sekhemkhet	2648–2640
Khaba	2640–2637
Huni	2637–2613
Dynasty 4 begins	2613
Sneferu	2613–2589
Cheops	2589–2566

Djedefra	2566–2558
Chephren	2558–2532
Menkaura	2532–2503
Shepseskaf	2503–2496
Dynasty 5 begins	2496
Userkaf	2496–2487
Sahura	2487–2475
Neferirkara	2475–2455
Shepseskara	2455–2448
Raneferef	2448–2445
Niuserra	2445–2421
Menkauhor	2421–2414
Djedkara	2414–2375
Unas	2375–2345
Dynasty 6 begins	2345
Teti	2345–2332
Pepi I	2332–2287
Merenra	2287–2278
Pepi II	2278–2184
Queen Nitiqret	2184–2181

First Intermediate Period

Dynasties 7 and 8 begin	2181
Wadjkara	?
Qakara Iby	?
Dynasties 9 and 10 begin	2160
Meryibra Khety	2160
Merykara	?

Middle Kingdom

Dynasty 11 begins	2130
Mentuhotep I	?
Intef I	2125–2112
Intef II	2112–2063
Middle Egyptian language develops	2100
Intef III	2063–2055
Mentuhotep II	2055–2004
Mentuhotep III	2004–1992
Mentuhotep IV	1992–1985
Dynasty 12 begins	1985
Amenemhet I	1985–1955
Senusret I	1965–1920

Amenemhet II	1922–1878
Senusret II	1880–1874
Senusret III	1874–1855
Amenemhet III	1855–1808
Amenemhet IV	1808–1799
Queen Sobekneferu	1799–1795
Dynasty 13 *begins*	1795
Wegaf	1795
Ameny Intef IV	1760
Hor	1760
Sobekhotep II	1750
Khendjer	1750
Dynasty 14 *begins*	1750
Sobekhotep III (dynasty 13)	1745
Neferhotep I (dynasty 13)	1740
Sobekhotep IV (dynasty 13)	1725
Ay (dynasty 13)	1720
Neferhotep II (dynasty 13)	?
Nehesy (dynasty 14)	?

Second Intermediate Period

Dynasty 15 begins	1650
Sheshi	1650
Yakhubher	?
Dynasty 16 begins	1650
Anather	?
Yaobaam	?
Dynasty 17 begins	1650
Intef VI(?)	?
Sobekemsaf II	?
Taa I	?
Khyan (dynasty 15)	1600
Late Egyptian language develops	1600
Taa II (dynasty 17)	1560
Kamose (dynasty 17)	1555–1550
Apepi I (dynasty 15)	1555
Apepi II (dynasty 15)	?

New Kingdom

Dynasty 18 begins	1550
Ahmose I	1550–1525

Amenhotep I	1525–1504
Tuthmosis I	1504–1492
Tuthmosis II	1492–1479
Tuthmosis III	1479–1425
Queen Hatshepsut	1473–1458
Amenhotep II	1427–1400
Tuthmosis IV	1400–1390
Amenhotep III	1390–1352
Akhenaten	1352–1336
Smenkhara	1338–1336
Tutankhamun	1336–1327
Ay	1327–1323
Horemheb	1323–1295
Dynasty 19 *begins*	1295
Ramesses I	1295–1294
Seti I	1294–1279
Ramesses II	1279–1213
Merenptah	1213–1203
Amenmesse	1203–1200
Seti II	1200–1194
Siptah	1194–1188

Queen Tausret	1188–1186
Dynasty 20 begins	1186
Setnakhte	1186–1184
Ramesses III	1184–1153
Ramesses IV	1153–1147
Ramesses V	1147–1143
Ramesses VI	1143–1136
Ramesses VII	1136–1129
Ramesses VIII	1129–1126
Ramesses IX	1126–1108
Ramesses X	1108–1099
Ramesses XI	1099–1069

Third Intermediate Period

Dynasty 21 begins	1070
Pinudjem I	1070–1032
Smendes I	1069–1043
Menkheperra	1045–992
Amenemnisu	1043–1039
Psusennes I	1039–991
Amenemope	993–984

Osorkon the Elder	984–978
Siamun	978–959
Psusennes II	959–945
Dynasty 22 begins	945
Sheshonq I	945–924
Osorkon I	924–889
Sheshonq II	c.890
Takelot I	889–874
Osorkon II	874–850
Takelot II	850–825
Harsiese	840
Sheshonq III	825–773
Dynasty 23 begins	818
Pedibastet	818–793
Sheshonq IV	c. 780
Osorkon III	777–749
Pimay (dynasty 22)	773–767
Sheshonq V (dynasty 22)	767–730
Dynasty 25 begins	747
Piankhi (dynasty 25)	747–716
Osorkon IV (dynasty 22)	730–715

Dynasty 24 begins	727
Tefnakht (dynasty 24)	727–720
Bakenrenef (dynasty 25)	720–715
Shabaka (dynasty 25)	716–702
Shabitko (dynasty 25)	702–690
Taharqo (dynasty 25)	690–664
Tanutamun (dynasty 25)	664–656

Late Period

Dynasty 26 begins	664
Psamtek I	664–610
Demotic language develops	650
Nekau II	610–595
Psamtek II	595–589
Wahibra	589–570
Ahmose II	570–526
Psamtek III	526–525
Dynasty 27 (First Persian Period) begins	525
Persia conquers Egypt	525
Cambyses II	525–522
Darius I	522–486

Xerxes I	486–465
Artaxerxes I	465–424
Darius II	424–405
Artaxerxes II	405–359
Dynasty 28 begins	404
Amyrtaeus	404–399
Dynasty 29 begins	399
Nefaarud I	399–393
Hakor	393–380
Dynasty 30 begins	380
Nakhtnebef	380–362
Djedhor	362–360
Nakhthorheb	360–343
Second Persian Period begins	343
Persia takes Egypt again	343
Artaxerxes	343–338
Arses	338–336
Darius III	336–332

Graeco-Roman Period

Alexander the Great takes Egypt	332

Alexander the Great	332–323
Foundation of Alexandria	331
Philip Arrhidaeus	323–317
Alexander IV	317–305
Ptolemaic dynasty begins	305
Ptolemy I	305–282
Ptolemy II	285–246
Ptolemy III	246–221
Ptolemy IV	221–204
Ptolemy V	204–180
Rosetta Stone is set up	196
Ptolemy VI	180–145
Ptolemy VII	145–144
Ptolemy VIII	145–116
Ptolemy IX	116–81
Ptolemy X	116–88
Ptolemy XI	80
Ptolemy XII	80–58, 55–51
Queen Berenice	58–55
Queen Cleopatra VII	51–30
Egypt becomes a Roman province	30

Royal Names

The names and titles of pharaohs developed over time. By 2000 BC they were known by a combination of five different names or titles (the 'fivefold titulary'), a form of aggrandisement and propaganda by which a pharaoh's role as ruler was stressed, as well as his right to the throne and his relationship with the gods. These five types of name became more or less standard for pharaohs after this time, but it is very rare to find all five of a pharaoh's names listed together in a text. The five different types of name are called:

Horus name
Nebti name
Golden Horus name
Throne name
Birth name

The Horus name is the earliest type of name and appears from around 3150 BC. At first it was the only name a pharaoh had. The name was contained within a *serekh*, ▯, a rectangular frame that represented a rectangular enclosure and the front of a mud-brick palace. The serekh was usually positioned vertically, and on top was placed the hieroglyph 𓅃, the symbol of the god Horus (see page 141), showing that the pharaoh was the incarnation of that god. *Serekh* was an Egyptian word for 'makes known', implying that this was how the pharaoh's name was made known. For a short period in dynasty 2 (around 2700 BC), the falcon was replaced by the symbol for the god Seth (see page 150), so this type of name became the Seth name instead of the Horus name (used by the pharaohs Peribsen and Khasekhemwy).

The Nebti name is sometimes called the 'Two Ladies' name and is preceded by the hieroglyph 🪶 ('nebti'), meaning 'two ladies'. The 'nebti' hieroglyph was the sign for the vulture goddess Nekhbet of Upper Egypt (see page 146) and the cobra goddess Wadjet of Lower Egypt (see page 154). It became a standard element of a pharaoh's name from dynasty 12, although it was used as early as dynasty 1.

The Golden Horus or Golden Falcon name was preceded by the hieroglyph 🦅 ('Horu-nebu'), meaning 'Golden Horus'. The significance of this sign is still disputed among Egyptologists, but possibly refers to the divinity of the pharaoh, with him representing the god Horus on earth.

The last two names of the pharaoh (the throne name and the birth name) were written in 'name rings' called cartouches, a French word meaning 'cartridges'. A cartouche, ◯, was an oval outline which literally represented a ring of rope. When the French invaded Egypt in 1798 they gave the word *cartouche* to these ovals, because to them they looked like the profile of their own field gun cartridges. The ancient Egyptian word for cartouche was 𓍢𓏤𓂝𓏲

('shenu'), meaning 'circle' or 'to encircle'. Originally it may have denoted that the pharaoh whose name was within the cartouche was ruler of everything encircled by the sun – the whole world. Later on it became customary to write the names of queens and royal children in cartouches as well. Foreign rulers of Egypt adopted the royal names, but generally only the ones in cartouches: a throne name and their own foreign birth name, but not the other three titles. It is the throne name and birth name that are most commonly seen on monuments, rather than the other three names. They are also the most easily noticed names, simply because they are written inside cartouches.

The throne name was also called the prenomen (from the Latin *praenomen*, 'forename'). It did not come into use until dynasty 5, but became the most important name of the pharaoh, often the only one mentioned in texts, and was adopted on his accession to the throne. This throne name often incorporated reference to the god Ra (page 149), whose sign ⊙ would be placed first out of reverence, even though the 'ra' element might be pronounced last. For example, the throne name of the pharaoh Senusret II was ⊙⌒𓎛, Khakheperra, and that of Queen Nitiqret was ⊙▭∪, Menkara.

The title 𓇓𓆤 ('nesu-bity', or 'nesut-bity') was generally placed before the throne name cartouche. The hieroglyph 𓇓 means 'sedge', but can also mean king, and the hieroglyph 𓆤 means 'bee' or 'honey' but can also mean 'king'. The title is commonly translated as 'King of Upper and Lower Egypt', because the sedge is the symbol of Upper Egypt and the bee the symbol of Lower Egypt. It also stood for 'King of the Dualities', a title with a range of complex interpretations reflecting the stark contrasts in Egypt, such as lush farmland and barren desert.

The fifth name of the pharaoh was his birth name, which was actually the first name given to him. It is today also called the nomen (from the Latin *nomen*, meaning simply 'name'), and the cartouche was preceded by the hieroglyphs 🦆 (Sa-Ra), meaning 'Son of Ra', emphasising the pharaoh's direct connection with the god Ra. Although the throne name was the one most commonly used in ancient Egyptian texts, pharaohs today are usually referred to by their birth name.

The combination of five names was unique to each pharaoh. Because many pharaohs were named after their ancestors, especially their fathers or grandfathers, many birth names were duplicated over time. There are, for example, several pharaohs with the name Ramesses and several called Tuthmosis. For this reason, the different pharaohs are today given numbers, such as Ramesses I and Ramesses II, although that was never the practice in ancient Egypt.

The two names in cartouches (the birth name and the throne name) are usually sufficient to identify a pharaoh, even where they shared the same birth name. For example, the pharaoh Tuthmosis I had the birth name 🦆(🦆) ('Born of Thoth [the god]'), which is exactly the same as the birth name of the next pharaoh, Tuthmosis II. However, the throne name of Tuthmosis I was ⚡(⚡), Aakheperkara, meaning 'Great is the Form of the Soul of Ra', whereas the throne name of Tuthmosis II was ⟨hieroglyphs⟩, Aakheperenra, meaning 'Great is the Form of Ra'. Even though the difference between ⟨hieroglyphs⟩ and ⟨hieroglyphs⟩ ⟨hieroglyphs⟩ is slight, it is enough to distinguish Tuthmosis I from his son Tuthmosis II.

One example of the full set of five names of a pharaoh is that of Amenemhet III, who ruled in dynasty 12 from 1855 to 1808 BC. He is numbered 'III', because he had the same birth name as Amenemhet I (who ruled 1985–1955 BC) and Amenemhet II (who ruled 1922–1878 BC). The son of Amenemhet III is in turn called Amenemhet IV.

Horus name: ⟨hieroglyphs⟩ (Aa-baw, meaning 'His Impressiveness is Great').

Nebti name: ⟨hieroglyphs⟩ (Iwat-tawy, meaning 'He Who Takes Possession of the Inheritance of the Two Lands').

Golden Horus name: ⟨hieroglyphs⟩ (Wahankh, meaning 'He Whose Life is Enduring').

Throne name: ⟨hieroglyphs⟩ (Nimaatra, meaning 'Belonging to the Justice of Ra').

Birth name: ⟨hieroglyphs⟩ (Amenemhet, meaning 'Amun is at the Head').

Later pharaohs from dynasty 18 often had adjectives accompanying these names in cartouches, such as Amenmesse, who has 'heqa-waset' ('ruler of Thebes') within the cartouche of his birth name, and Seti II, who has 'merenptah' ('beloved of Ptah') within the cartouche of his birth name.

The spelling of the names of pharaohs can vary and there is no absolutely correct system, because hieroglyphs are being translated into English, so that Amenhotep can appear as Amenhotpe or even the ancient Greek version Amenophis, while Ramesses can also appear as Ramses or Rameses.

Meanings of Names

Names of people, especially the various names of the pharaohs, could be spelled out using the uniliteral hieroglyphs (see page 35), such as Teti, , which is actually tti, but for convenience the letter 'e' is placed between the two 't's. These names do not seem to have a particular meaning, while the meaning of many others can be worked out, such as in the throne name of Pepi I, which is Meryra, meaning 'Beloved of Ra' – that is to say, 'Beloved of the God Ra'.

Within the names of pharaohs, Ra, Amun, Sobek, Thoth, Ptah, Horus, Montu and Seth are the names of gods. 'Ra' is often part of a pharaoh's throne name, but in English this can be spelled as either 'ra' or 're', such as Neferkara or Neferkare. Another example is the throne name of the pharaoh Merykara, composed of ⊙ ('ra,' referring to the god Ra), ∊ ('mer', meaning 'beloved' or 'loved'), 𐎧𐎧 (the letter 'y'), and ⊔ ('ka', meaning 'soul'). This spells the name Rameryka, but to make sense, this is written in English as Merykara, which can be translated as 'Beloved is the Soul of Ra' or as 'The Soul of Ra is Loved'. Very often in Egyptian names, the name of a god is placed first in a sequence of hieroglyphs out of reverence for the god.

The birth name of the pharaoh Amenhotep I is written as ⟨◻◻◻◻◻⟩. ◻ is the letter 'i'. ◻ is the biliteral sign for 'mn', written in English for convenience as 'men' and usually meaning 'everlasting', although here it is used to spell out the word 'imen'. In English this word 'imen' is more usually written as 'amen' or 'amun' and means the god Amun. The sign ﹍ is also part of the name of Amun: it is the letter 'n', used here a phonetic complement (see page 32) to make the letter 'n' in 'men' quite clear and not to give another 'n'. The second part of the pharaoh's birth name is ◻◻, a group of signs representing the word 'htp', which is more conveniently written in English as 'hotep'. This word can be translated as 'offering', 'content' or 'pleased'. In names, 'hotep' can appear simply as ◻. The last two signs in this name are the letters 't' (◻) and 'p' (◻), which are phonetic complements, simply emphasising those two letters in 'hotep'. The name Amenhotep therefore means 'Amun is content'.

Some words which form the most common parts of names are:

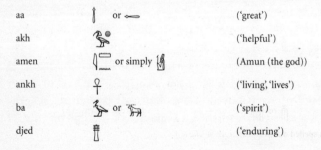

aa	or	('great')
akh		('helpful')
amen	or simply	(Amun (the god))
ankh		('living', 'lives')
ba	or	('spirit')
djed		('enduring')

djeser		('holy')
em	or	('at' or 'in')
en		('of or 'belongs to')
hedj		('bright')
heqa		('ruler')
het or hat		('first', 'foremost')
hor or har		(Horus (the god))
hotep or hetep	or	('offering', 'content', 'pleased')
ib		('heart')
iunu		(Heliopolis (the town))
ka		('soul')
kha		('appears', 'appearance')
kheper		('appearance', 'form', 'come into being')
khet	often abbreviated as	('body')
maat	or or or	('justice', 'truth')
men		('eternal')
mer or mery	or or or	('beloved', 'love')
mes	or	('born of', 'formed by')

(quite often spelled out in translations as 'mose')

mi		('like')
nakht	or	('strong')
neb		('lord')
nefer		('beautiful')
netjer		('divine', 'god')
nub		('golden', 'gold')
per		('home', 'house')
ptah		(Ptah (the god))
ra	or	(Ra (the god))
sekhem		('powerful', 'power')
setep		('chosen')
sheps	or	('noble')
si or sa	or	('son')
sobek	or	(Sobek (the god))
tawy		('the two lands')
user		('powerful')
wadj		('flourishing')
wah		('always', 'endures')
waset		(Thebes (the city))

A Few Famous Pharaohs

For those pharaohs whose names frequently occur in books and museum exhibits, some information is given here on their names, as well as a little family history, their dynasty (see page 81), and their burial place at death. It will be obvious that many of the pharaohs married and had children by their own sisters, half-sisters and daughters, an unacceptable and illegal practice today but normal then in order to keep the royal blood line pure. The names of the pharaohs given here, with hieroglyphs and translations where known, are those that were contained either in serekhs or cartouches (see page 96) – usually the birth name and throne name. They are shown without their title of ⟨Sa-Ra⟩ (Sa-Ra) and ⟨nesu-bity⟩ (nesu-bity). Many pharaohs also had three other names, which are explained under 'Royal Names' on page 95.

If known, the present whereabouts of the pharaoh's mummy and coffins is given. Many pharaohs were buried in the Valley of the Kings at Thebes, but their tombs were constantly plundered for the treasure they contained, and so the priests collected and hid some of the mummies with their coffins. Many centuries later, two hidden caches of royal and high-status mummies were found, one in 1881 with over forty mummies, and another in 1898 with around fifteen mummies. The word 'mummy' comes from the Arabic *mumia* ('mineral pitch'), and until the nineteenth century crushed and powdered mummy was recommended as medicine for various ailments; the demand became so great that fake mummies were manufactured using bodies that had only been dead a few years! Most pharaohs were buried in a nest of wooden coffins inside a stone coffin (which is usually called a sarcophagus).

Ahmose I (or Ahmosis). Birth name: Ahmose ('Born of the Moon'). Throne name: Nebpehtyra ('Ra is the Lord of Strength'). His father was the pharaoh Taa II and his mother Queen Aahotep. By his principal wife and sister Ahmose Nefertari, he had a son who became the pharaoh Amenhotep I and a daughter Ahmose who married the pharaoh Tuthmosis I. His other wives were Kasmut and Inhapi and his other children included a son called Siamun. Ahmose was probably buried in the Dra Abu El-Naga area of Thebes, but the location of his tomb is unknown, although his mummy was in the cache found in 1881 and is now in the Cairo Museum along with his coffin. He reigned for twenty-five years, 1550–1525 BC, in dynasty 18, possibly initially with Queen Aahotep as co-regent. He died at about the age of thirty-five.

Akhenaten. Originally called Amenhotep IV, he adopted the birth name Akhenaten ('Servant of Aten'), because he restricted royal worship to the sun god Aten only. Birth name: Amenhotep ('Amun is Content'). Adopted birth name: Akhenaten

('Servant of Aten'). Throne name: Neferkheperura-waenra ('Beautiful are the Forms of Ra, Unique One of Ra'). His father was the pharaoh Amenhotep III and his mother Queen Tiy. His chief wife was Nefertiti (the daughter of his chief minister Ay and therefore not of royal blood). Other wives were Merytaten (his own daughter, who became his chief wife after the death of Nefertiti), Kiya, Mekytaten and Ankhesenpaaten (his own daughter, who after his death became the pharaoh Tutankhamun's wife). Akhenaten was possibly the father of one daughter and of a son Tutankhamun by his wife Kiya, and he had six daughters by Nefertiti including Merytaten, Mekytaten and Ankhesenpaaten. He was possibly the father of Merytaten-tasherit (Merytaten the Younger) by his own daughter and wife Merytaten and possibly the father of another daughter by his own daughter and wife Ankhesenpaaten. Akhenaten was probably buried at his new capital Akhetaten ('Horizon of the Aten', today known as El-Amarna), where fragments of his stone sarcophagus have been found, which are now in the Cairo Museum. He was later reburied in the Valley of the Kings, and the male mummy discovered in tomb KV55 (originally identified as Queen Tiy) may be his. He reigned for sixteen years, 1352–1336 BC, in dynasty 18, possibly with his younger brother Smenkhara as co-ruler for the last two years.

Amenemhet I (or Amenemhat or Ammenemes). Birth name: Amenemhet ('Amun is at the Head'). Throne name:

Sehetepibra ('The Heart of Ra is Satisfied'). He was of non-royal rank, the son of a priest by the name of Senusret and a woman by the name of Nofret. He himself was the chief minister of the previous pharaoh, Mentuhotep IV. Amenemhet had several wives, and he introduced the practice of co-regency, sharing the throne in the last years of his reign with his eldest son Senusret I. He set up a new royal burial ground at El-Lisht, where he was buried in a pyramid after his assassination, but the burial chamber is now below water level. He reigned for thirty years, 1985–1955 BC, in dynasty 12.

Amenemhet II (or Amenemhat or Ammenemes). Birth name: Amenemhet ('Amun is at the Head'). Throne name: Nubkaura ('The Souls of Ra are Golden'). His father was the pharaoh Senusret I and his mother was Nefru. His principal wife was Mereryet, and he had several daughters, as well as a son who became the pharaoh Senusret II. He was buried in a pyramid at Dahshur, which still contains his stone sarcophagus. He reigned for forty-four years, 1922–1878 BC, in dynasty 12, in part with his father and later with his own son.

Amenemhet III (or Amenemhat or Ammenemes). Birth name: Amenemhet ('Amun is at the Head'). Throne name:

Nimaatra ⬚ ('Belonging to the Justice of Ra'). His father was the pharaoh Senusret III and his mother was Sebekshedty-Neferu. He had a daughter called Neferu-Ptah and his son became the pharaoh Amenemhet IV. He built a pyramid at Dahshur, but was buried in another pyramid at Hawara, in front of which were so many courts and shrines that it gave rise to the legend of the labyrinth. Stone sarcophagi survive in both pyramids. He reigned for forty-six years, 1855–1808 BC, in dynasty 12.

Amenhotep I (or Amenhotpe or Amenophis). Birth name: Amenhotep ⬚ ('Amun is Content'). Throne name: Djeserkara ⬚ ('Holy is the Soul of Ra'). His father was the pharaoh Ahmose I and his mother was Ahmose-Nefertari. His wives were Aahotep II and Ahmose-Merytamun, but he had no heir as his only son died young. Amenhotep's tomb was in the Dra Abu El-Naga area of Thebes. His mummy was in the cache found in 1881 and still has a face mask. Now in the Cairo Museum, it remains the only royal mummy not to have been unwrapped in modern times. He reigned for twenty-one years, 1525–1504 BC, in dynasty 18, probably initially with his mother and in his last years with Tuthmosis I.

Amenhotep II (or Amenhotpe or Amenophis). Birth name: Amenhotep (with the title heqa-iunu) ⬚ ('Amun is Content', with the title 'Ruler of Heliopolis'). Throne name: Aakheperura

⟨hieroglyphs⟩ ('Great are the Forms of Ra'). His father was the pharaoh Tuthmosis III and his mother Hatshepsut-Merytra (not to be confused with the pharaoh Queen Hatshepsut). His wives were his sister Merytamun as well as Tio, by whom he had a son who became the pharaoh Tuthmosis IV. Amenhotep was buried in tomb KV35 in the Valley of the Kings, where his stone sarcophagus was found with his mummy which had been partly rewrapped by priests after ancient tomb robbing. His sarcophagus is still in the tomb, but the mummy (six feet tall) has been moved to the Cairo Museum. The priests also used his tomb to hide a cache of other royal mummies, which were rediscovered in 1898. He is the only pharaoh to be found still in his sarcophagus within his own tomb, apart from Tutankhamun. He reigned for twenty-seven years, 1427–1400 BC, in dynasty 18.

Amenhotep III (or Amenhotpe or Amenophis). Birth name: Amenhotep (with the title heqa-waset) ⟨hieroglyphs⟩ ('Amun is Content', with the title 'Ruler of Thebes'). Throne name: Nebmaatra ⟨hieroglyphs⟩ ('Ra is Lord of Truth'). His father was the pharaoh Tuthmosis IV and his mother Queen Mutemwiya. He had numerous wives, many from diplomatic marriages, but his chief wife Tiy was of non-royal rank, a daughter of a noble called Yuya and his wife Tjuiu, who outlived him. By Tiy he had at least two sons and four daughters: the elder son died, and the younger one became the pharaoh Amenhotep IV (later changing his name to Akhenaten). Amenhotep III also married two of his own daughters, Isis and Sitamun. He was buried in tomb WV22 in the Valley of the Kings, which was robbed in ancient times although fragments of a stone sarcophagus are still in the tomb. His mummy was in the cache found in 1898 and is now in the Cairo Museum. He reigned for thirty-eight years, 1390–1352 BC, in dynasty 18, initially with his mother as co-ruler. He may have been about forty-five years of age at his death.

Cheops (or Khufu or Kheops or Suphis I). Birth name: Khufu (An abbreviation of Khnum-khuefui, 'Khnum [a god] Protects Me'). His father was the pharaoh Sneferu and his mother Hetepheres I. Cheops married an unknown queen, then Meritates, Henutsen and another unknown queen. He had numerous sons and daughters, the sons including the later pharaohs Djedefra and Chephren. He was buried in the Great Pyramid at Giza, which remained the tallest building in the world until the nineteenth century, and his stone sarcophagus (empty on discovery) is still in the burial chamber (the King's Chamber). He reigned for twenty-three or twenty-four years, 2589–2566 BC, in dynasty 4.

Chephren (or Khafra or Rakhaef or Khephren or Suphis II). Birth name: Khafra ('Appearing like Ra'). His father was the pharaoh Cheops and his mother was probably Henutsen. His wives included Meresankh III and Khamerernebty I. His sons included the later pharaoh Menkaura (by Khamerernebty I), and he had one daughter. He built the Great Sphinx at Giza (a massive lion with

Chephren's head), as well as the Second Pyramid where he was buried. His plain polished stone sarcophagus was found sunk into the floor of the burial chamber. He reigned twenty-four to twenty-six years, 2558–2532 BC, in dynasty 4.

Djoser (or Zoser or Tosorthos). Birth name: possibly Djoser. Horus name: Netjerikhet [hieroglyphs] ('Divine Body'). He was the son of the pharaoh Khasekhemwy and brother of the pharaoh Sanakht. His wife was Hetephernebty, who was possibly his sister. He was buried in the Step Pyramid at Saqqara, which was built as a series of six steps by his chief minister and architect Imhotep – the first monumental stone building in the world. A mummified left foot and other mummy fragments were found in the burial chamber. He reigned for nineteen years, 2667–2648 BC, in dynasty 3.

Hatshepsut (a female pharaoh). Birth name: Hatshepsut-Amun [hieroglyphs] ('Foremost of Noble Ladies, Amun'). Throne name: Maatkara [hieroglyphs] ('Truth is the Soul of Ra'). Her father was the pharaoh Tuthmosis I and her mother was Queen Ahmose. She married her half-brother Tuthmosis II and had only one child, a daughter called Neferura. She was portrayed in art with all the trappings of a pharaoh, including the royal false beard. She prepared a tomb for herself to the west of the Valley of the Kings, where a stone sarcophagus was found unused, but instead was buried in the Valley of the Kings, sharing tomb KV20 with her father Tuthmosis I. Two stone sarcophagi, one for her (now in the Cairo Museum) and one for Tuthmosis I (now in the Museum of Fine Arts, Boston, USA), were found in the KV20 tomb. Her mummy has not been found. She also had a huge mortuary temple dedicated to the god Amun at Deir El-Bahari, built by the architect Senenmut. She reigned alongside Tuthmosis II and III, but pushed her stepson Tuthmosis III to one side from 1473 BC until her death or overthrow in 1458 BC. She reigned for fifteen years, 1473–1458 BC, in dynasty 18.

Horemheb (or Horemhab or Haremhab). Birth name: Horemheb (with the title meryamun) (☐☐☐☐☐) ('Horus is Jubilant' with the title 'Beloved of Amun'). Throne name: Djeserkheperura-sete-penra (☐☐☐) ('Holy are the Forms of Ra, Chosen by Ra'). He was an army officer under previous pharaohs. His family came from Heracleopolis, but his parents are unknown. After the death of the pharaoh Ay, he declared himself king. He had two unknown wives as well as Mutnodjmet, possibly a sister of Nefertiti (the wife of the pharaoh Akhenaten). He replaced all the names of the two previous pharaohs, Ay and Tutankhamun, with his own. He was buried in the Valley of the Kings, in tomb KV57, but had earlier prepared a private tomb for himself at Saqqara. His stone sarcophagus is still in KV57, but his mummy has not been found. The mummy of a female with a newborn child found in his tomb may have been his wife Mutnodjmet; Horemheb died without an heir. He reigned for twenty-eight years, 1323–1295 BC, in dynasty 18.

Menkaura (or Mycerinus or Mencheres). Birth name: Menkaura ('The Souls of Ra are Eternal'). His father was the pharaoh Chephren and his mother was Khamerernebty I. He married two unknown queens as well as his sister Khamerernebty II. He had two sons and one daughter. He was buried in the Third Pyramid at Giza, and his decorated and lidless stone sarcophagus was found in the burial chamber, inside which was a wooden coffin. His burial chamber was robbed in ancient times, and so a new wooden coffin was made for him around 650 BC. The sarcophagus was lost at sea in the nineteenth century on its way to the British Museum in London, but the wooden coffin along with parts of the mummy did reach the museum. He reigned for twenty-nine years, 2532–2503 BC, in dynasty 4.

Mentuhotep II (or Mentuhotpe). Birth name: Mentuhotep ('Montu is Content'). Throne name: Nebhepetra (possible meaning 'Pleased is the Lord Ra'). His father was the pharaoh Intef III and his mother was Yah or Aoh. His many wives included Tem and his sister Neferu. His son by Tem became the pharaoh Mentuhotep III. Mentuhotep II was buried behind his mortuary temple at Deir El-Bahari in Thebes. Only fragments of a coffin and some bones of the mummy have survived and are now in the British Museum in London, but his stone sarcophagus is still in the tomb. He reigned for fifty-one years, 2055–2004 BC, in dynasty 11.

Merenptah (or Merneptah). Birth name: Merenptah (with the title hetep-her-maat) (𓇓𓏏𓆑𓏤...) ('Beloved of Ptah', with the title 'Truth is Joyful'). Throne name: Baenra-merynetjeru (⊙𓏤...) ('The Spirit of Ra, Beloved of the Gods'). He is often thought to be the pharaoh of the Exodus, but for no good reason. He was the thirteenth son of the pharaoh Ramesses II and his mother was Queen Istnofret. His wives were Istnofret and Takhat. His son was Seti-Merenptah who became the pharaoh Seti II. He was buried in the Valley of the Kings, in tomb KV8, in a nest of three stone sarcophagi, one inside the other. The innermost one was removed to Tanis for the burial of the pharaoh Psusennes I (and is now in the Cairo Museum), and parts of the other two sarcophagi are still in tomb KV8. His mummy was in the cache found in 1898 and is now in the Cairo Museum. He reigned for ten years, from when he was in his sixties, 1213–1203 BC, in dynasty 19.

Narmer (possibly also called Menes). Horus name: Narmer 𓃒𓆟𓏏𓏤 ('The Striking Catfish'). This pharaoh's name appears on many objects, and he himself is depicted on a carved piece of green slate (the Narmer Palette, in the Cairo Museum) and on a macehead (the Narmer Macehead, in the Ashmolean Museum, Oxford): he wears the White Crown (*hedjet*) of Upper Egypt on the palette and the Red Crown (*deshret*) of Lower Egypt on the macehead. He is possibly the same pharaoh known as Menes and the father of the pharaoh Aha. He may have been buried in a royal cemetery at Abydos. He reigned around 3100 BC, in dynasty 1.

Pepi I (or Pepy or Piopi or Phiops). Birth name: Pepi (ㅁㅁ૧૧). Throne name: Meryra (☉⤬૧૧) ('Beloved of Ra'). His father was the pharaoh Teti and his mother was Iput. His wives were Ankhnesmerire I and II (daughters of a nobleman from Abydos: they were both given the same name) and Weret-Imtes (who unsuccessfully plotted to assassinate him, and was probably executed). His sons by Ankhnesmerire I and II were Merenra and Pepi II (both would become pharaohs), and his daughter was called Neith. He was buried in a pyramid at south Saqqara, which still contains his stone sarcophagus. Only one of his mummified hands has survived and is now in the Cairo Museum. He reigned for forty-five years, 2332–2287 BC, in dynasty 6, probably from a young age.

Pepi II (or Pepy or Piopi or Phiops). Birth name: Pepi (ㅁㅁ૧૧). Throne name: Neferkara (☉⟟∪) ('Beautiful is the Soul of Ra'). His father was the pharaoh Pepi I and his mother was Ankhnesmerire II. His numerous wives included his sister Neith. He was buried in a pyramid at south Saqqara, which still contains his stone sarcophagus. He reigned for ninety-four years, 2278–2184 BC, in dynasty 6, from the age of six, the longest-reigning monarch in history.

Pinudjem I (or Pinedjem). Birth name: Pinudjem (with the title meryamun) (⟨⟞⟰𖤍⟩) ('He who belongs to the Pleasant One', with the title 'Beloved of Amun'). Throne name: Khakheperrasetepenamun ('The Appearance of Ra Comes into Being, Chosen by Amun'). As High Priest of the god Amun at Thebes, he ruled an area from Aswan to just south of the delta. His father was Piankh, a high priest and general. His wives were Henuttawy I (a daughter of the pharaoh Ramesses XI) and his own daughter Maatkara. By Henuttawy he had four children: his daughter was Maatkara and one son became the pharaoh Psusennes I, while two other sons, Masaherta and Menkheperra, both became high priests at Thebes. Pinudjem's mummy, now in the Cairo Museum together with his coffins, was in the cache found in 1881. It is not known where he was originally buried, but he reused the coffins of Tuthmosis I. He reigned for thirty-eight years, 1070–1032 BC, in dynasty 21.

Psamtek I (or Psammetichus I). Birth name: Psamtek . Throne name: Wahibra ('The Heart of Ra is Enduring'). His father was Nekau I, pharaoh of Sais, and one of his daughters was Nitiqret. His son became the pharaoh Nekau II. Psamtek began by ruling Egypt on behalf of the conquering Assyrians, but by the ninth year of his reign he had become an independent ruler of Upper and Lower Egypt. He defeated his opponents in the delta using mercenary soldiers from Greece. He reigned for fifty-four years, 664–610 BC, in dynasty 26.

Ramesses II (or Ramses or Rameses – and is also known as Ramesses the Great). Birth name: Ramesses (with the title meryamun)

('Ra has Formed Him', with the title 'Beloved of Amun'). Throne name: Usermaatra-setepenra ('The Justice of Ra is Powerful, Chosen by Ra'). His father was the pharaoh Seti I and his mother was Tuya. He had numerous wives; his eight main wives were Nefertari (his first and favourite, buried in tomb QV66 in the Valley of the Queens), Istnofret, Bint-Anath (his daughter by Istnofret), Merytamun (his daughter by Nefertari), Nebettawy (his daughter), Henutmira (his younger sister), Maathorneferura and one of unknown name. He had well over 100 children. His sons by Nefertari included Amenhirkhopshef. His sons by Istnofret included Ramesses, Khaemwaset and Merenptah (who became the next pharaoh). His daughters included Merytamun, Bint-Anath and Nebettawy. He was possibly the pharaoh of the Exodus, when the Hebrews under the leadership of Moses escaped from slavery in Egypt to the Promised Land. Ramesses II was buried in the Valley of the Kings, in tomb KV7, but only a few of the contents survive, and are now in the British Museum in London, the Louvre in Paris, Berlin Museum, and Brooklyn Museum (USA). His mummy was in the cache found in 1881 and is now in the Cairo Museum. He reigned for sixty-six years from the age of twenty-five, 1279–1213 BC, in dynasty 19.

Ramesses III (or Ramses or Rameses). Birth name: Ramesses (with the title heqa-iunu) ('Ra has Formed Him', with the title 'Ruler of Heliopolis'). Throne name: Usermaatra-meryamun ('The Justice of Ra is Powerful, Beloved of Amun'). His father was the pharaoh Setnakhte and his mother was Tiy-Meren-ese. Little is known of his wives and children. His wives included Isis (the chief queen), Titi (possibly his daughter) and Tiy (who plotted to murder him and was probably executed). He also had many minor wives and numerous children, including at least ten sons, but many died before him and were buried in the Valley of the Queens. They included Khaemwaset, Parahirwenemef, Sethirkhopshef, Amenhirkhopshef, and the later pharaohs Ramesses IV (possibly by Titi), Ramesses V and Ramesses VI (by Isis). His daughter was called Titi. He was buried in the Valley of the Kings, in tomb KV11, which was discovered in 1769 by James Bruce. The tomb has paintings of two blind harpists and is often called 'The Tomb of the Harpers' or 'Bruce's Tomb'. His stone sarcophagus is in the Louvre in Paris and the sarcophagus lid is in the Fitzwilliam Museum, Cambridge. His mummy was in the cache found in 1881 and along with a wooden coffin is in the Cairo Museum. He reigned for thirty-one years and forty-one days, 1184–1153 BC, in dynasty 20.

Senusret I (or Senwosret or Sesostris). Birth name: Senusret ('He of Wosret [a goddess]'). Throne name: Kheperkara ('The Soul of Ra Comes into Being'). His father was the pharaoh Amenemhet I and his mother was Nefrytatenen. Senusret's chief wife was Nefru, by whom he had a son who became the pharaoh Amenemhet II. His daughters were Itekuyet and probably Nefru-Sobek, Nefru-Ptah and Nenseddjedet. He was buried in a pyramid at El-Lisht, but only a leg bone has been found. He reigned for forty-five years, 1965–1920 BC, in dynasty 12, in part with his father and later with his own son.

Senusret II (or Senwosret or Sesostris). Birth name: Senusret (⟦🝋⟧) ('He of Wosret [a goddess]'). Throne name: Khakheperra ⟦🝋⟧ ('The Form of Ra Appears'). His father was the pharaoh Amenemhet II and his mother was Nefru. His principal wife was Nofret. His son became the pharaoh Senusret III. He was buried in a pyramid he built at El-Lahun, where the burial chamber still contains an empty stone sarcophagus. He reigned for six years, 1880–1874 BC, in dynasty 12, in part with his father.

Senusret III (or Senwosret or Sesostris). Birth name: Senusret (⟦🝋⟧) ('He of Wosret [a goddess]'). Throne name: Khakaura ⟦🝋⟧ ('The Souls of Ra Appear'). His father was the pharaoh Senusret II. He had several wives, including Mereret and possibly his sister Sit-Hathor. His sons included the pharaoh Amenemhet III. Senusret was buried in a pyramid at Dahshur, which still contains his sarcophagus. He reigned for nineteen years, 1874–1855 BC, in dynasty 12.

Seti I (or Sety or Sethos). Birth name: Seti (with the title meryenptah) ⟦🝋⟧ ('He of Seth', with the title 'Beloved of

Ptah'). Throne name: Menmaatra ('Eternal is the Justice of Ra'). His father was the pharaoh Ramesses I and his mother was Sitra. His wife was Tuya (the daughter of a military lieutenant) who died in her sixties and was buried in the Valley of the Queens. He had two sons by Tuya; one died young and one became the pharaoh Ramesses II. His daughters were Tia and Henutmira (who married her brother Ramesses II). Seti I was buried in the Valley of the Kings, in tomb KV17, the longest and deepest tomb in the valley. Seti's mummy was in the cache found in 1881 and is now in the Cairo Museum, along with a coffin. His stone sarcophagus is in the Soane Museum in London. He reigned for fifteen years, 1294–1279 BC, in dynasty 19.

Sheshonq I (or Sheshonk or Shoshenk or Shishak). Birth name: Sheshonq (with the title meryamun) (the title 'Beloved of Amun', with the foreign name Sheshonq). Throne name: Hedjkheperra-setepenra ('The Form of Ra is Bright, Chosen by Ra'). He was a nephew of the pharaoh Osorkon the Elder and a general under the pharaoh Psusennes II whose daughter he married. He had several sons, including Iuput, Djedptahaufankh, Nimlot and the pharaoh Osorkon I. He is the Shishak mentioned in the Bible as undertaking conquests in Judah and Israel and taking away treasure from cities in the region including Jerusalem. The location of his tomb is unknown. He reigned for twenty-one years, 945–924 BC, in dynasty 22.

Sneferu (or Snefru or Snofru or Soris). Birth name: Sneferu ('He of Goodness'). His parents were the pharaoh Huni and probably Huni's minor wife Meresankh I. Sneferu married his half-sister Hetepheres, who was his principal wife. Their son became the pharaoh Cheops. Sneferu moved the royal burial ground to Dahshur, where he built two pyramids: the Bent Pyramid and a mile away the first true pyramid known as the Red (or North) Pyramid, where parts of his mummy were found. He reigned for twenty-four years, 2613–2589 BC, in dynasty 4.

Teti. Birth name: Teti . His origins are unknown, but his wives included Iput, who was a daughter of the pharaoh Unas, and Khuit. He had a son by Iput who became the pharaoh Pepi I and a daughter named Seshseshet (who married the chief minister Mereruka). Teti may have been murdered by his bodyguard, and he was buried in a pyramid at north Saqqara. His lidless stone sarcophagus is still in the pyramid's burial chamber, and a wooden coffin is in the Cairo Museum, along with a few fragments of his mummy. He reigned for thirteen years, 2345–2332 BC, in dynasty 6.

Tutankhamun (or Tutankhamen or Tutankhamon). Birth name: Tutankhaten ('Living Image of Aten'). Adopted birth name: Tutankhamun (with the title heqa-iunu-shema) ('Living Image of Amun', with the title 'Ruler of Upper Egyptian Heliopolis'). Throne name: Nebkheperura ('Ra is Lord of Forms'). This pharaoh is especially famous because his spectacular tomb was discovered almost intact in 1922 by Howard Carter and Lord Carnarvon, although it had been broken into twice in ancient times. His mother was possibly Queen Kiya and his father was possibly the pharaoh Akhenaten. His wife was his half-sister Ankhesenpaaten (who later changed her name to Ankhesenamun). He had no sons, although two mummies found in his tomb were probably stillborn daughters. He was buried in a nest of coffins in tomb KV62 of the Valley of the Kings, a small tomb that was possibly the only one available at the time of his sudden death. The huge number of objects from the tomb are now in the Cairo Museum, including the inner coffin of sheet gold, the middle wooden gilded coffin and the inlaid gold mask covering the mummy. Other objects are in Luxor Museum, while in the tomb are preserved the stone sarcophagus, the outermost wooden gilded coffin and the mummy. He reigned for nine years from about the age of nine, 1336–1327 BC, in dynasty 18.

Tuthmosis I (or Thutmose or Djehutymes). Birth name: Thutmose 𓅱𓏏𓁟 ('Born of Thoth'). Throne name: Aakheperkara 𓇳𓆣𓂝𓏤 ('Great is the Form of the Soul of Ra'). He was a general of the pharaoh Amenhotep I. His wife was Queen Ahmose, who was the daughter of the pharaoh Ahmose I and Queen Ahmose Nefertari. His two elder sons, Wadjmose and Amenmose, predeceased him. A younger son, by his minor wife Mutnefert, became the pharaoh Tuthmosis II. His elder daughter by Queen Ahmose became the pharaoh Hatshepsut. He was the first pharaoh to be buried in the Valley of the Kings, in tomb KV38. A stone sarcophagus was found in the tomb and is now in the Cairo Museum, while another was found in KV20, the tomb of Hatshepsut, where his mummy may have been transferred. His mummy has not been found, but his coffin is in the Cairo Museum. He was co-ruler with Amenhotep I and then reigned for twelve years, 1504–1492 BC, in dynasty 18.

Tuthmosis II (or Thutmose or Djehutymes). Birth name: Thutmose ('Born of Thoth'). Throne name: Aakheperenra ('Great is the Form of Ra'). His father was the pharaoh Tuthmosis I and his mother was Mutnefert. He married his half-sister Hatshepsut. He had one son, Tuthmosis III, by his minor wife Isis, and a daughter, Neferura, by Hatshepsut. He was possibly buried in tomb KV42 in the Valley of the Kings which still contains an undecorated sarcophagus. His mummy was in the cache found in 1881 and is now in the Cairo Museum. He reigned for thirteen years, with Hatshepsut as co-ruler, 1492–1479 BC, in dynasty 18, until his death in his early thirties.

Tuthmosis III (or Thutmose or Djehutymes). Birth name: Thutmose ('Born of Thoth'). Throne name: Menkheperra ('Eternal is the Form of Ra'). His father was the pharaoh Tuthmosis II and his mother was Isis. His wives were Neferura (his half-sister, who died before he came to the throne), then Hatshepsut-Meryetra (of non-royal rank and his principal queen), and several minor ones such as Menhet, Menwi and Merti. His son (by Hatshepsut-Merytra) became the pharaoh Amenhotep II. Because of his numerous military campaigns and because he was a short man, he has been described as the 'Napoleon of ancient Egypt'. He was buried in tomb KV34 in the Valley of the Kings, which still contains the stone sarcophagus. His mummy was in the cache found in 1881, in its original outer wooden coffin, and is now in the Cairo Museum. He reigned for fifty-four years, 1479–1425 BC, in dynasty 18, although his aunt and stepmother Hatshepsut initially acted as regent and then took over his power from 1473 BC until she died or was overthrown in 1458 BC. Later in his reign Tuthmosis erased all memory of her by physically obliterating her name on many monuments.

Tuthmosis IV (or Thutmose or Djehutymes). Birth name: Thutmose ('Born of Thoth'). Throne name: Menkheperura ('Eternal are the Forms of Ra'). His mother was Queen Tio and his father was the pharaoh Amenhotep II. His son by one of his chief wives, Queen Mutemwiya, became the pharaoh Amenhotep III. He was buried in tomb KV43 in the Valley of the Kings, which still contains his stone sarcophagus. His mummy was in the cache found in 1898 and is now in the Cairo Museum. He reigned for ten years, 1400–1390 BC, in dynasty 18.

Unas (or Wenis or Unis). Birth name: Unas . His wives included Nebet and Khenut. One daughter was Iput who married

The Little Book of Egyptian Hieroglyphs

the pharaoh Teti. Unas had no heir. He was buried in a pyramid at north Saqqara, the earliest to have its internal walls inscribed with spells of the Pyramid Texts. Parts of his mummy were found in the pyramid and are now in the Cairo Museum. His stone sarcophagus is still in the pyramid. He reigned for thirty years, 2375–2345 BC, in dynasty 5.

Royal Crowns

A pharaoh could be depicted wearing a number of different crowns, which also appear as hieroglyphic signs:

The White Crown, ⟨glyph⟩ (*hedjet*), was the earliest form of crown, often called the Crown of Upper Egypt (the south). It is seen as early as the reign of the pharaohs Scorpion and Narmer. The crown was sometimes called the Nefer or the White Nefer and was occasionally depicted in a similar way to the hieroglyph ⟨glyph⟩ for 'nefer', meaning 'good' or 'beautiful'.

The Red Crown, ⟨glyph⟩ (*deshret*), is often called the Crown of Lower Egypt (the north). As a hieroglyph, it was commonly used to write the letter 'n', as an alternative to ⟨glyph⟩.

The Double Crown, ⟨glyph⟩ (*pschent*), was formed by the white and red crowns combined and was worn by pharaohs of the unified state of Upper and Lower Egypt.

From dynasty 18 pharaohs also wore the Blue Crown (*khepresh*), ⟨glyph⟩, which at times is referred to as the war crown.

The Atef Crown, ⟨glyph⟩, comprised a crown with double feathers and a ram's horns. It was worn by the pharaoh in certain religious rituals.

Time and the Seasons

Dates were written according to the particular year of reign of the current pharaoh, giving the regnal year, the month, season and day, and then the pharaoh's throne name, such as 'year two, second month of the inundation, day one under the majesty of the pharaoh Khakaura' ⟨hieroglyphs⟩.

The Egyptians divided the year into twelve months, and the months into thirty days, with three ten-day weeks per month. The year therefore consisted of 360 days, and so to bring the number up to 365, five days were added at the end of the year that were regarded as the birthdays of the deities Osiris, Isis, Horus, Seth and Nephthys.

The night was divided into twelve hours and the daytime into twelve hours, the word for 'an hour' being ⟨hieroglyphs⟩, 'unut'. The length of the hours would vary from season to season, as daytime began with sunrise. The word for 'morning' or 'tomorrow' was ⟨hieroglyphs⟩, 'dua'. 'Today' was ⟨hieroglyphs⟩, 'min'. 'Night' was ⟨hieroglyphs⟩, 'gereh', and 'day' was ⟨hieroglyphs⟩, 'heru'.

The year was divided into three seasons (rather than the four seasons of spring, summer, autumn and winter found in Europe). The seasons were tied in with the annual flooding of the River Nile (the inundation), which no longer occurs as the water is now held back artificially in Lake Nasser by the Aswan Dam. The name for the inundation was 𓇳, 'hapy' (the same name that was given to the god of the Nile – see page 139).

The year began in mid-July when the annual inundation began, and that season was called 𓇳, 'akhet', which lasted to mid-November. Then came the growing season, 𓇳, known as 'peret', which lasted to mid-March, then the harvest season, 𓇳, 'shemu'.

Body and Soul

The ancient Egyptians thought that the world was inhabited by three types of conscious beings: living people, 𓋹𓈖𓐍𓀀𓏥 ('ankhu'); gods, 𓊹𓊹𓊹 ('neteru'); and the akhs, 𓅜𓏤 ('akhiu'), who were spirits of the ancestors. The Egyptians believed that each human being was made up of five elements, every one of which was necessary for existence. These elements were the body, 𓏤𓄿 ('ha'), the shadow, 𓇳𓏤 ('shut'), the ba, 𓅡 ('ba'), the ka, 𓂓 ('ka'), and the name, 𓂋𓈖𓀁 ('ren').

The body was obviously an essential part of each person, and the shadow was regarded as an important extension of the body; in the bright light of Egypt, shadows are ever-present. Their name was also considered to be an essential part of a person, and someone whose name was destroyed or lost ceased to exist. Because of this, many people tried to ensure that their name would continue to exist after they died by carving or painting it on their coffin, tomb and anywhere else it might survive. Sometimes the names of people, including pharaohs, would be systematically erased in an attempt to destroy them in the afterlife.

The ba is part of the person that is difficult to define precisely. It was a spirit of the person that was in part made up of their personality; the ba was the element that made each person an individual, and it was believed to live on after the death of the person. It is often portrayed as a human-headed bird in Egyptian art and as a hieroglyph showing a human-headed bird with an offering of a pot of smoking incense in front of it: 🜨. The final element that went to make up each person was the ka. Like the ba, the ka is also difficult to define but approximated to the person's soul or 'life-force', and it too was believed to live on after a person's death.

Although the ba and the ka were believed to live on after death, admittance to the afterlife was not automatic. What ancient Egyptians feared most was the 'second death' that resulted in oblivion if a person failed to obtain the afterlife, and consequently many religious rituals and magic spells were used to try to ensure that a person did not suffer this second death. It was believed that when a person died their ka was automatically separated from their body, but the ba was not. The person's body was preserved by mummification, and various rituals were performed to free the ba from the body, so that it could join the ka. Once the ba had joined the ka, the dead person became an akh 🜊 and could live on in the afterlife.

Before the ba could join the ka, however, the dead person had to face final judgement by the gods. The person's heart was weighed to see if they had led a just and proper life, and only if the decision was in their favour could they survive. Because this judgement was considered so important, collections of spells such as the Book of the Dead were largely concerned with ensuring that the dead person gave all the right answers and so passed the tests, as well as trying to provide an easy life for the dead person in the afterlife.

Once the dead person had become an akh, they continued to live as a spirit among the living, rejoining their mummy each night and sleeping in their tomb to emerge in the daytime and enjoy life free from the burdens of physical existence. Akhs were thought to live on the same plane as the gods and have some god-like powers, but they could also derive nourishment from food which was placed as offerings in mortuary chapels; they were believed to be able to extract the nourishing essence from such offerings, leaving the actual food apparently untouched. They were also thought to be able to assist the living, and letters written to the dead and posted in tombs often asked for such help.

Gods and Goddesses

Before writing developed in Egypt, and so literally before history, each small community within the Nile Valley had its own group of gods and goddesses. Over the centuries, as Egypt became united, some gods and goddesses merged where it was seen that their function was the same and only their names were different. For example, in the hot sunny climate of Egypt, the sun was worshipped as a god in most places, but had different names. This process of merging gradually reduced the number of gods and goddesses, but tended to take place only in adjacent areas. Priests and the local people were probably reluctant to let their own deities be replaced by ones from far away. Even so, Egypt still had a large number of gods and goddesses, mostly worshipped within quite limited areas of the country; very few were worshipped throughout the country.

All the gods and goddesses had their own myths and legends, although in the merging of deities some myths and legends were mixed together, while several minor gods and goddesses survived as elements of other more important gods and goddesses. These attempts at rationalising Egyptian religion were not entirely successful, leaving several different groups of major gods worshipped in different cities in Egypt, with conflicting myths and legends, while many minor local and household gods were honoured by small shrines and statues rather than in grand and impressive temples.

A collection of major gods was called ⦿𓏤𓏤𓏤𓀭 (Pesedjet) by the Egyptians, but Egyptologists now use the term *ennead*, which is derived from the ancient Greek word for 'nine', even though most enneads do not consist of exactly nine deities! The Heliopolitan Ennead, the centre of whose cult was at the city of Heliopolis, consisted of the creator god Atum and his son Shu and daughter Tefnut whose marriage produced a son Geb and a daughter Nut. The marriage of Geb and Nut produced two sons, Osiris and Seth, and two daughters, Isis and Nephthys. These nine deities are sometimes known as the Great Ennead.

Another group of deities was called 𓏥𓏥 𓆓𓆓𓁐𓀭 (Khemnyu), meaning 'the eight gods', although Egyptologists now use the term *ogdoad*, derived from the ancient Greek word for 'eight'. The group was made up of four frog-headed gods and four snake-headed goddesses who were thought to have ruled before the creation of the world. Pairs of gods and goddesses represented different aspects of the primeval chaos that existed before the emergence of the sun god: the god Nun and the goddess Nunet represented the primeval ocean, the god Heh and the goddess Hehet represented infinite space, Kek and Keket represented darkness, and Amun and Amunet represented hidden power or invisibility. This last group was especially popular at Hermopolis.

Through the gradual merging of many local gods and goddesses, some came to be worshipped throughout the Nile Valley, and yet Egypt never had a universal system of religion, no sacred books like the Bible or the Koran, and no religious dogma. Religion was part of daily life, with no hard divisions, as there are today, between religion, magic, superstition, medicine or science. Religious rituals were regarded as having practical and immediate effects, such as maintaining the cycle of the seasons, making the sun shine, avoiding the collapse of order, curing illness and ensuring life after death.

In the following alphabetical list of gods and goddesses, their names are given in hieroglyphs. Sometimes these deities are better known today not by their Egyptian name, but by a later form of their name (usually ancient Greek). So for Anubis, for example, the original ancient Egyptian name of Inpu is given as well. The hieroglyphs 𓆓 and 𓃀 are determinatives (see page 31) for 'god' or 'divine', and can occur at the end of a hieroglyphic name, which shows the reader that this is definitely the name of a god or goddess.

Amun or the single hieroglyph. Recognisable by the two high plumes on his crown, Amun was also linked with the fertility god Min, as Amun-Min, in which case he is portrayed with an erect penis. He was also linked with the sun god Ra, as Amun-Ra, when he is portrayed as wearing a sun disc as well as plumes on his crown. The main animal sacred to Amun was the ram, and so the god was sometimes portrayed with a ram's head.

His name Amun means 'the hidden one', and he was thought of as the invisible force in the wind. Originally one of the primeval gods of the ogdoad, Amun became associated with the reigning pharaoh. From dynasty 11 he was a god of Thebes and rose in importance to become the supreme god of the Egyptians. Later, the ancient Greeks equated him with their chief god Zeus.

Anubis (literally 'Inpu') or the single hieroglyph. This god can also be portrayed as a crouching jackal, with the hieroglyph used on its own to represent the name Anubis in hieroglyphic texts. He usually appears as a man with the head of a jackal, but he was not the only jackal-headed god worshipped by the Egyptians. Originating in Upper Egypt as a god of the dead, Anubis was eventually regarded throughout Egypt as the god who presided over cemeteries and burial rituals and who protected the dead on their journey to the afterlife.

Apis 𓇓𓂝𓃒𓏏 (literally 'Hapu'). Represented as a bull with a sun disc on his head, Apis was believed to be the god Ptah living on earth in the form of a bull. At the temple of Ptah in Memphis a sacred bull was kept, worshipped and consulted as an oracle. When the bull died it was mummified and buried at Saqqara in a huge underground complex, now known as the Serapeum, and another sacred bull was found. The bull that was selected would have either a white crescent on one side of its body, a white crescent on its forehead, a black vulture-shaped patch on its back, or a black spot under its tongue.

Apophis 𓏺𓏺𓆙 (literally 'Apep'). Represented as a huge serpent, Apophis was the snake god of the underworld. He was the indestructible and eternal enemy of the sun, and every night he attacked the sun as it journeyed through the underworld from the west to the east. Every night Apophis had to be defeated so that the sun could rise again. He symbolised the forces of darkness and evil that were constantly at war with the forces of goodness and light.

Aten 𓇋𓏏𓈖𓇳𓏥 (literally 'Aten-Ra'). Aten was a sun god very closely connected with the sun god Ra. Aten was considered to be the disc of the sun (the body of Ra) and was portrayed as a sun disc with a uraeus (representing the goddess Wadjet) and with rays radiating from the disc which ended in hands. During the reign of the pharaoh Akhenaten all the gods were abandoned in favour of a religion based solely on the worship of Aten, but at the death of Akhenaten the situation was reversed and Aten once more became one god among many.

Atum ▱. Represented as a man wearing the combined crowns of Upper and Lower Egypt, or wearing the royal headdress, Atum can be confused with portraits of pharaohs. He was the creator god who emerged from the primeval waters (symbolised by the god Nun) to create Shu and Tefnut whose marriage produced the rest of the gods and goddesses. Atum was seen as the father of the pharaoh, and after death a pharaoh would return to Atum. Atum protected the pharaoh and others in the underworld.

Bastet ▱. Originally represented as a woman with the head of a lion, and so easily confused with other lioness goddesses (Mut, Sekhmet, Tefnut), from about 1000 BC Bastet was portrayed as a woman with the head of a cat. Having started as a lioness goddess, she became a cat goddess and was very popular in Lower Egypt. As a lioness goddess she symbolised the anger of the sun god Ra, but as the cat goddess she was a protector of pregnant women and of people against disease and demons, as well as being a goddess of music, dancing and pleasure.

Bes 〿. Represented as a grotesque deformed dwarf, Bes was in fact a kindly god offering protection in all situations, in particular protection of women in childbirth and of the family. Bes had no temples of his own but appears on the walls of temples of other gods and was worshipped at home. His bizarre appearance was to frighten away evil spirits.

Geb 〿. A primeval god of the earth, Geb was portrayed as a man with a crown, but sometimes a goose, on his head. He was also regarded as a god of fertility, and in this role he was sometimes shown green in colour and with an erect penis. In the creation myth at Heliopolis, Geb was the son of Shu, god of the air, and of Tefnut, the goddess of moisture. Most gods in Egypt were thought to be children resulting from the marriage of Geb and his sister Nut, the sky goddess. Geb frequently appears in scenes connected with funerary rituals, being separated from his sister Nut by their father Shu.

Hapy (or Hapi) 〿. Represented as a long-haired naked man with a large paunch and hanging breasts, often with a crown of water plants, and pouring water from an urn, Hapy was the god of the annual Nile flood (the inundation). There were no temples dedicated to Hapy, but he is often portrayed on the walls of temples dedicated to other gods. Another god also called Hapy was one of the Sons of Horus – see page 151.

Hathor [hieroglyphs] but more usually the single hieroglyph [hieroglyph] or [hieroglyph]. One of the most important goddesses, Hathor was represented in various forms: as a woman with cow horns and a sun disc on her head (a form similar to one of those of Isis); as a cow; and as a pillar in a temple, at the top of which is carved a woman's face with the ears of a cow. Hathor was a sky goddess, but also a protector of cemeteries, a goddess of the dead, and a goddess of love, as well as presiding over fate, healing, music and dance. She was believed to be the wife of Horus.

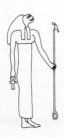

Heket (sometimes called Heqat) [hieroglyphs]. Portrayed as either a frog or a woman with a frog's head, Heket was a goddess of childbirth, fertility and regeneration of plant life.

Horus ⬚⬚🕊 but more usually the single hieroglyph 🕊. Represented as a falcon or as a man with the head of a falcon, Horus was one of the oldest and most important gods in Egypt. His main roles were as a sky god and a sun god, but he was also protector of the pharaoh (who was considered to be Horus alive on earth) and a symbol of perfection. Horus had many forms such as Harpocrates (Horus as a child), Harakhty (Horus of the horizon, a sun god), and Harendotes (Horus the avenger of Osiris). In myth, Horus was the son of Osiris and fought with

the god Seth after he had killed Osiris. Images of Horus are seen throughout Egypt, and the various myths about him and his varying functions in different places are very complex and difficult to unravel.

Imhotep 🕊⬚. An official, architect and high priest of Ptah who served four pharaohs in dynasty 3, he was responsible for several buildings including the Step Pyramid of the pharaoh Djoser (see page 112). He became so famous that about 2,000 years after his death he was regarded as a god. He was revered as a god of knowledge and healing and was portrayed as a seated man with a shaven head (the mark of a priest), with an open papyrus scroll on his knees.

Ipy ⬚⬚⬚🕊 . Portrayed as a hippopotamus, Ipy was a protective goddess, particularly of the royal family, but also of mothers and children. In her form and function she is almost indistinguishable from the goddess Taweret.

Isis ⌐ or ⌐ (literally 'Iset'). Usually portrayed as a woman with the symbol of a throne on her head, Isis is sometimes seen as a woman wearing a crown with cow horns and a sun disc in a form that is easily confused with some of the representations of the goddess Hathor. Isis was one of the most important goddesses in Egypt, a mother goddess thought to possess immense magical powers. In myth she was the sister and wife of Osiris and the mother of Horus. Since the pharaoh was regarded as the god Horus living on earth, Isis was called the mother of the pharaoh.

Khepri ⌐ or ⌐ (literally 'Kheperer'), but often the single hieroglyph ⌐. Portrayed as a dung beetle (scarab) or as a man with a dung beetle for a head, Khepri was a form of the sun god Ra. The image of the dung beetle was commonly used as an amulet to symbolise the sun god and to provide protection for the person wearing it.

Khnum ⌇ 𓆟 ⌇ 𓃶 or the single hieroglyph 𓃗 or 𓃺 .
Portrayed as a man with the head of a ram, and
sometimes wearing a sun disc and plumes on his
head, Khnum can be confused with the sun god Ra.
Khnum was a creator god, originally worshipped at
Elephantine in Upper Egypt. He came to be
regarded as guardian of the source of the Nile and
controller of its floods. He was also associated with
Ra.

Khonsu 𓈖 𓆓 𓄿 𓅂 . A moon god and a god of war,
Khonsu was represented in several different ways: as
a mummified child standing upright, with one side
lock of hair (the fashion for children) and holding
the royal crook and flail sceptres; as a youth with the
head of a falcon, on top of which is a combination
of a crescent and a moon disc; and as a baboon (in
which form he can be confused with Thoth).
Originally a violent god of war, Khonsu developed
into a god of healing and came to be regarded as the
son of Amun and Mut.

Maat ⟫⟞⟝𓁐 or the single hieroglyph 𓁐 or 𓆄. Portrayed as a woman with a single ostrich feather in her hairband, or sometimes just by the feather itself, Maat was the goddess of cosmic harmony and personified truth and justice. In portrayals of judging the dead, to see if they were eligible for the afterlife, the dead person's heart was weighed against Maat's feather 𓆄. If the scales did not balance, the dead person could not enter the afterlife. In myth, Maat was the wife of Thoth.

Meretseger ⟝⟞⟝𓁐𓆗. Represented as a coiled cobra or as a cobra with the head of a woman, Meretseger was a local goddess of the mountain that overlooks the ancient cemetery of the Valley of the Kings at Thebes. She was a cobra goddess who protected the royal tombs at Thebes and came to be regarded as a goddess of the whole of Thebes.

Min ⟝⟞𓁐 or the single hieroglyph 𓁦. Min was usually portrayed as a man with an erect penis and both arms raised (he appears to have only one arm in some pictures), holding a flail and wearing a plumed headdress. He was the god of sexual activity and fertility and was sometimes linked with the god Amun.

Montu ⬚ or sometimes the single hieroglyph. Represented as a man with the head of a falcon, on top of which are two plumes with a sun disc and uraeus (representing the goddess Wadjet), Montu was a god of war. A white bull with a black face, called Buchis, was worshipped as Montu alive on earth at the city of Hermonthis.

Mut ⬚ or the single hieroglyph. Usually represented as a woman wearing a headdress in the shape of a vulture, on top of which was the double crown of Upper and Lower Egypt, Mut is sometimes shown as a woman with the head of a lion and so can be confused with the other lioness goddesses (Bastet, Tefnut, Sekhmet). Mut was a sky goddess and a goddess of war, but was also associated with the cat goddess Bastet.

Nefertum ⬚. Portrayed as a man with a lotus blossom on his head, or occasionally as a man with a lion's head, Nefertum was the god of rebirth that was symbolised by the lotus. In myth he was the son of Ptah and Sekhmet.

Neith ⬚ or the single hieroglyph. Represented as a woman with bows and arrows, or simply as two crossed arrows tied up in a package (of which

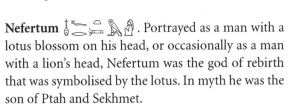

the hieroglyph  is a much simplified version), Neith was the goddess of war. Originally a local goddess of Sais in the Nile Delta, Neith developed into a goddess known throughout Egypt and was regarded as the wife of the god Seth. Because her symbol of crossed arrows was mistaken for a weaving shuttle, she later became the goddess of weavers.

Nekhbet 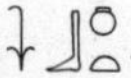. Represented as a vulture, Nekhbet was the goddess of Upper Egypt. She came to symbolise that part of the country and was often portrayed with the goddess Wadjet to symbolise the unity of Upper and Lower Egypt. In this respect, Nekhbet sometimes appears alongside the uraeus (representing the goddess Wadjet) on the headdress of the pharaoh, to show that he ruled the whole of Egypt.

Nephthys  (literally 'Nebethut') or the single hieroglyph . Portrayed as a woman with the hieroglyphs meaning 'the lady of the mansion' on her head, Nephthys was a funerary goddess who protected the pharaoh in the underworld. In myth she was the wife of Seth, but she seduced Osiris, and Anubis was their son.

Nun . A primeval god of water, Nun symbolised the original watery abyss from which the creator sun god Atum emerged. Nun is portrayed as a man, with no instantly recognisable identifying marks.

Nut ⬭⬭⬭. Usually shown as a woman, Nut was occasionally portrayed as a cow. She was a primeval sky goddess. In the creation
myth at Heliopolis, Nut was the daughter of Shu, god of the air,
and of Tefnut, the goddess of moisture. Most of the gods in Egypt
were thought to be children resulting from the marriage of Nut and
her brother Geb. Nut frequently appears in scenes connected with
funerary rituals, being separated from her brother Geb by their
father Shu.

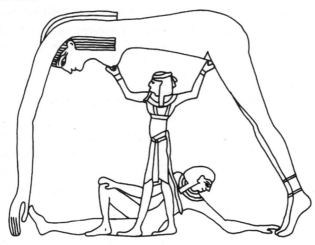

The Little Book of Egyptian Hieroglyphs

Osiris 𓊨𓏤𓀭 (literally 'Wsir' or 'Usir'). One of the most important gods of Egypt, Osiris was represented as a mummified man standing upright, holding the royal crook and flail and wearing a tall crown with two plumes. He was the supreme god of the dead and ruled over the underworld. He was also a god of resurrection and the judge of the dead, deciding who was admitted to the afterlife. In myth, Osiris was brother and husband of Isis and was killed by their brother Seth, but brought back to life by Isis. Osiris was closely associated with Ptah and Sokar, and the association became so strong that the three gods were virtually interchangeable.

Ptah 𓊪𓏏𓎛 or the single hieroglyph 𓁰 or 𓁰. The most distinguishing feature of Ptah was his smooth shaven head, and he was usually portrayed as a mummified man standing upright and holding a sceptre. At Memphis he was considered to be a creator god, but he became known throughout Egypt as a god of architects, artists and craftsmen. He was also a funerary god, closely associated with Osiris and Sokar, and this association became so strong that they were virtually interchangeable.

Ra or Re ⌢🔲⊙🧍 or as the single hieroglyph 🧍 or 🧍.
The hieroglyph ⊙ represents the sun and was also
used to represent the god Ra. It is often seen in the
names of pharaohs in cartouches. The most common representation of Ra was as a falcon with a sun
disc on its head, leading to confusion with some
representations of Horus, with whom Ra was in any
case closely linked. Ra was also portrayed as a sun
disc being rolled along by a scarab (dung beetle),
and when portrayed in the underworld he took the
form of a man with the head of a ram, on top of
whose horns was a sun disc. Originally worshipped
as a creator god at Heliopolis, Ra became the most
popular sun god in Egypt. See also Khepri on page
142.

Sekhmet 👁️⊙. Portrayed as a woman with the
head of a lion, and often with a sun disc on her
head, Sekhmet was a lioness goddess of Memphis.
She can sometimes be confused with other lioness
goddesses (Bastet, Mut, Tefnut). Sekhmet came to
be regarded as the daughter of the sun god Ra and
the wife of the god Ptah. Her name means 'powerful', and she represented the destructive power of
the sun, although she was also thought to be a
powerful sorcerer and healer.

Seshat |⎯ 𓏤 △ . Represented as a woman wearing a panther-skin robe and a seven-pointed star on top of a stick on her head, Seshat was a goddess of writing and recording, concerned with accounts, measurement of time and the laying out of building foundations. Often seen with writing implements or a tally-stick, in myth she was the wife of the god Thoth.

Seth 𓊃𓏏𓐠𓃩 or the single hieroglyph 𓁣 or 𓃩 . Represented as the 'Seth animal' (𓃩), an imaginary creature similar to a jackal, or as a man with a 'Seth animal' head, the god Seth was the embodiment of evil. In myth, Seth killed his brother Osiris and usurped the throne. Seth was eventually defeated by Horus, the son of Osiris. Seth came to be regarded as lord of the desert and of non-Egyptian lands. He took up a position in the solar boat, which was used by the sun to travel through the underworld each night, and helped to fight off attacks from the serpent Apophis. He also controlled the weather.

Shu 𓈙𓅱𓀭 . Represented as a man with a plume on his head, or occasionally as a man with the head of a lion, Shu was a primeval god of the air. In the creation myth at Heliopolis, he was the son of the creator god Atum. He married his sister Tefnut, the goddess of moisture, and had a son Geb (the earth) and a daughter Nut (the sky).

Sobek  . Portrayed as a man with a crocodile head or as a crocodile with two plumes on its head, Sobek was a crocodile water god. In some myths his sweat made up the waters of the River Nile.

Sokar  . Portrayed as a man with the head of a hawk, Sokar was a god of the dead at the cemetery for the city of Memphis at Saqqara. He became associated with Ptah and Osiris, and so from a local god he developed into one worshipped throughout Egypt. The association between Osiris, Ptah and Sokar became so strong that they were virtually interchangeable.

Sons of Horus. These were four gods called **Imsety** , **Duamutef** , **Hapy** and **Qebehsenuef** . They were four funerary gods who protected specific organs removed from the body during mummification. Imsety was portrayed as a man and looked after the liver; Duamutef was portrayed as a jackal and looked after the stomach; Hapy took the form of a baboon and was guardian of the lungs; and Qebehsenuef was represented as a hawk and protected the intestines. The organs were often stored in sets of four jars called Canopic Jars, the lids of which were made to look like the heads of the four Sons of Horus.

Sothis (literally 'Sopdet'). Represented as a woman wearing a tall crown with a five-pointed star on top, Sothis personified the star Sirius. Because the bright appearance of Sirius in the dawn sky in July marked the start of the inundation – the annual flooding of the River Nile – Sothis was known as the herald of the New Year and the Nile flood.

Taweret . A hippopotamus goddess who protected women in childbirth, Taweret (meaning 'the great one') was usually represented in a grotesque form, shown as a female hippopotamus with human breasts. Her back, tail and part of her head were those of a crocodile, she had the feet of a lion and wore a wig of straight hair. Her bizarre appearance was only to frighten off evil spirits, and she was essentially a kindly goddess. In her form and function she is almost indistinguishable from the goddess Ipy.

Tefnut ⌒ ∿ ⌒ ᒋ . Represented as a lioness or as a woman with the head of a lion, Tefnut can be confused with other lioness goddesses (Bastet, Mut, Sekhmet). Tefnut was a primeval goddess who personified moisture. In the creation myth at Heliopolis, Tefnut was the daughter of the creator god Atum. She married her brother Shu, the god of sunlight and air, and had a son Geb (the earth) and a daughter Nut (the sky).

Thoth 🦩📜 (literally 'Djhuty') or the single hieroglyph 📜. Represented as an ibis or as a baboon, but most frequently as a man with the head of an ibis, and often shown writing on papyrus, Thoth was the scribe of the gods. He was an important god throughout Egypt and had several other roles. He was the god of knowledge and wisdom as well as of scribes, and so he became the protector of priests and physicians. Thoth was believed to have invented hieroglyphs and writing, but he was also concerned with numbers. As 'reckoner of the years' he was thought of as 'lord of time'. He was a god of the moon as well, and was sometimes regarded as a god of the dead.

Wadjet 𓆑𓏏𓇋𓆗 . Usually represented as a cobra rearing up to strike, the goddess Wadjet is occasionally also shown as a woman with a lion's head and can be confused with Sekhmet. Wadjet was the local goddess of the town of Buto in the Nile Delta, but became the goddess of Lower Egypt. She is the cobra frequently shown on the pharaoh's forehead as part of his headdress; this image of a cobra is now generally called the uraeus (from a Greek word *ouraios*, 'of a tail') and the Egyptians believed it symbolised a supernatural force ready to strike down enemies of the pharaoh. The uraeus was sometimes accompanied on the pharaoh's headdress by a vulture representing Nekhbet, the goddess of Upper Egypt.

Wepwawet 𓃢𓏤𓏤𓀭 . A jackal god, often portrayed as a jackal-headed man like Anubis. Originally a god of Upper Egypt, his name means 'opener of the ways', and he was regarded as a guide of the dead through the underworld. In funeral rituals the more widely known god Anubis took over the role of Wepwawet because he was easily confused with him.

Wosret 𓏏𓇋𓊃𓏏 . A local goddess of Thebes who is mainly known because some pharaohs from Thebes included her name (which means 'powerful') as part of their own name.

A Few Place Names

The ancient Egyptians had several names for their country, and these names reveal what they considered was important about the region where they lived. Egypt was ⌇⌇⌇ (Ta Meri), 'The Land of the Hoe', because it was agriculture that made Egypt rich. The Nile Valley, where most Egyptians lived, was ⌇⌇⌇ (Kemet), 'The Black Land', because the silt from the annual flooding of the River Nile fertilised the surrounding fields and turned the soil a dark colour which contrasted with the surrounding desert which was called ⌇⌇⌇ (Deshret), 'The Red Land'. The most common name for Egypt, though, was ⌇⌇⌇ (Tawy), 'The Two Lands', signifying Upper and Lower Egypt.

For most of its history Egypt was united, but there continued a memory of a time when the Nile Valley was divided into two countries that were later united, and the Egyptians still recognised differences between the southern part of the country, ⌇⌇⌇ (Ta Shemau), 'Upper Egypt', and the region of the Nile Delta in the north, ⌇⌇⌇ (Ta Mehu), 'Lower Egypt'. To the Egyptians, south was 'up' and north was 'down'. The River Nile, whose annual flooding was essential for successful crops and the continued existence of Egypt itself, was called ⌇⌇⌇ (Hapy). In flood, the Nile was

𓁸𓏏𓈖 (Hapy), which is a plural form of the name of the river.

When reading about Egypt or visiting the country, place names can be quite bewildering. Many places in Egypt have been occupied for thousands of years, during which time their names have changed, particularly as Egypt has been conquered successively by the Assyrians, Persians, Greeks, Romans, Arabs and Ottoman Turks. For example, the ancient Egyptian city of 𓉸𓅓𓏏𓊖 (Shabet) became Kainopolis under Greek rule and Maximianopolis under the Romans. The Copts called it Kournah and it is now a large city usually known as Qena. The ancient names of some sites are not yet known (if they ever had a name), and so these tend to be referred to by their modern name. Sometimes only the Greek and Roman names are known, not the earlier ancient Egyptian names, so such sites can be referred to by these or even their modern name.

A final source of confusion with place names is the often wildly different ways modern Egyptian (Arabic) names are spelled in English: for example, Madinat al-Fayyum and Medinet El-Faiyum are the same place, as is Sakkara and Saqqara. There are no rules governing which name should be used for which place; in the following list the ancient name of each place (often the ancient Greek name) is usually the one most commonly used today. The second column gives the modern Arabic name, while the last two columns give the ancient Egyptian name – in hieroglyphs and in transliteration (see page 25). The hieroglyph 𓊖 is a determinative (see page 31) meaning 'town' or 'settlement', so in the following place names it shows that these were the names of settlements.

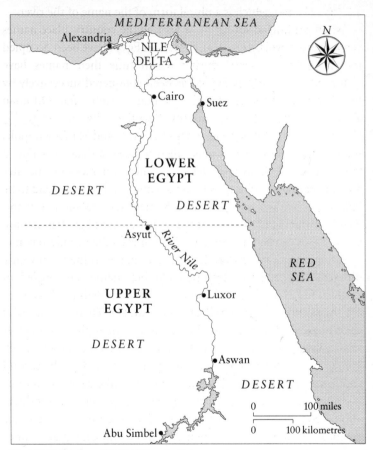

The Nile Valley from Abu Simbel to the Delta

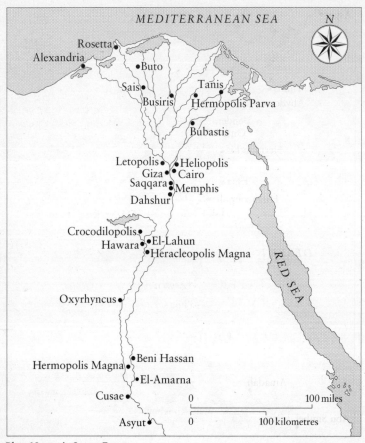

Place Names in Lower Egypt

Place Names in Upper Egypt

Ancient Name (mainly Greek/Roman)	Modern Name	Ancient Egyptian Hieroglyphic Name	Ancient Egyptian Name (Transliteration)
–	Abu Simbel		
			Per Ramesses Meryamun Pa Demi
Abydos	El-Araba El-Madfina		Abju
Akhetaten	El-Amarna		Akhet-Iten
Apollinopolis Magna	Edfu (or Idfu)		Djeba
Bubastis	Tell Basta		Baset
Busiris	Abusir (or Abu Sir Baria)		Dedu
Buto	Tell El-Farain		Pe
Coptos	Qift		Gebtiu
Crocodilopolis	Medinet El-Faiyum		Shejet
Cusae	El-Qusiya		Kis
Eileithyiaspolis	El-Kab		Nekheb
Heliopolis	Tell Hisn		Iunu

Heracleopolis Magna	Ihnasya El-Medina		Neni-Nesut
Hermonthis	Armant		Iuny
Hermopolis Magna	El-Ashmunein		Wenu
Hieraconpolis	Kom El-Ahmar		Nekhen
Kainopolis	Qena		Shabet
Latopolis	Esna		Iunyt
Letopolis	Ausim		Khem
Lycopolis	Asyut		Zaut
Memphis	Mit Rahina		Men-Nefer
Mendes	Tell Er-Ruba		Jedet
Ombos (north of Luxor)	Kom Ombo		Nebyt
Ombos (south of Luxor)	Tukh		Nebet
Oxyrhynchus	El-Bahnasa		Per-Mejed
Sais	Sa El-Hagar		Zau
Syene (Elephantine)	Aswan		Abu
Tentyris	Dendera		Iunet

Thinis	Girga		Thini

(the ancient site has not yet been precisely located, and may even have been at nearby Birba)

Thebes (Diospolis Magna)	Luxor		Waset

162

Making Sense of Inscriptions

It is one thing to attempt to translate a hieroglyphic text in a quiet room, surrounded by dictionaries and reference books, with unlimited time to spare. It is quite another to try to make sense of an inscription on a monument in Egypt or on one of the thousands of Egyptian objects in museums around the world, with limited time to spare.

Even though pocket dictionaries of hieroglyphs do not yet exist as something handy to carry on such excursions, it is still possible to make some sense of an inscription without being an expert. The best approach is to look for clues rather than try for a word-by-word translation:

- Decide which way the hieroglyphs should be read: are they in horizontal lines or do they seem to be in vertical columns? And which way are they facing: 𓅱 or 𓅯?

- Look for clues giving the ends of words, such as determinatives (like 𓀁, 𓃀, 𓆓 and 𓁐), which occur at the end of words. The plural sign ııı or ¦ is easy to spot and will also mark the end of a word.

- Look at what the determinatives mean. Apart from indicating the ends of words, determinatives can also give clues to the meaning of those words. For example, 𓀀 shows a prisoner, indicating that the associated word is something to do with an enemy; 𓀁 indicates something to do with the mouth, such as speaking, and so on.

- Look for familiar phrases or familiar groups of hieroglyphs, such as 𓊪𓏤 and 𓊪𓏥 .

- Look for names in cartouches, such as 𓍹𓇳𓏠𓈖𓍺 . Identify the signs accompanying the cartouches 𓅓𓏤 , 𓇓𓏏 , so that you will know if you are looking at a birth name or throne name, or both.

- Become familiar with the hieroglyphs for the names of gods and goddesses, as well as the appearance of these deities in art. Many gods and goddesses look very similar in artistic representations (such as Hathor and Isis) and some can even look like pharaohs, so it is essential to be able to recognise their distinguishing features and read their names.

- Look for the hieroglyphs for numbers: this may give a clue as to the content of the inscription. Many scenes in temples depict offerings being presented to gods, with the numbers of gifts listed.

- Make sure you know the difference between what is art and what is an accompanying inscription. Because hieroglyphs are pictures of things, anyone unfamiliar with hieroglyphs can be confused between the hieroglyphic writing and the artistic representations: writing almost always accompanied pictures and often encroaches on parts of a picture.

The Last Word

Whatever aspect of ancient Egypt you next explore, you will probably encounter various formulaic phrases on monuments in Egypt and in museums. A handful of the more common ones are given here to help you tackle inscriptions.

Expressions about Life

A common formula, already seen in abbreviated form (see page 79), is 𓋹𓍑𓋴. In full, this is 𓋹𓈖𓐍 𓍅𓂝𓆓𓋴𓃀, 'ankh udja seneb', which means 'life, prosperity, health' (or 'may he live, be prosperous and healthy'), often abbreviated by Egyptologists to 'lph'. In this phrase, 𓋹 is the triliteral 'ankh', and ⁓ and ⊜ are phonetic complements, reinforcing the 'n' and 'kh' in 'ankh'. 𓍅 is the uniliteral 'u' or 'w' and 𓍑 is the biliteral 'dja', with 𓂝 (the uniliteral for 'a') acting here as a phonetic complement to reinforce the 'a' in 'dja'. 𓏤 is a determinative placed after words that are abstract ideas. The final part of the phrase is spelled with uniliterals: 𓊃 for 's', ⁓ for 'n' and 𓃀 for 'b', which spells 'snb', easier to pronounce in English if written as 'seneb'.

Parts of this formula are seen alongside the names of pharaohs, including ⚱️☥, 'ankh djet', which means 'living forever', with ☥ used again for 'ankh'. ☍ is a uniliteral for 'dj' and ⌒ is a uniliteral for 't', while ▭ is a determinative in words related to eternity. It can also be written as △☥☍, 'di ankh djet', 'given life forever'.

Another phrase used after the names of pharaohs is △☥, 'di ankh', 'given life', as well as △☥╫↑, 'di ankh djed was', 'given life, stability and power'. These phrases became so common that they could themselves be used as nouns, such as in ⌓△☥╫↑, 'so that he [the pharaoh] might achieve given life, stability and power'.

Offering Formula

Numerous hieroglyphic texts, especially on funerary tablets (stelae) and coffins, begin with what is today variously called the 'offering formula', 'dedicatory formula' or 'hotep-di-nesu formula'. This is the start of a prayer to enable the ka (soul) of the dead person in the afterlife to have a share of the offerings made by the king (that is, the pharaoh) to the gods at temples, especially during festivals.

The formula begins with ⟊⌂△ (sometimes written as ⟊△⌂), 'hotep-di-nesu', meaning 'an offering which the king gives' (in other words, 'a royal offering'), and is followed by the name of the god and a list of the provisions requested.

The word for 'king' ('nesu'), written as ⧣⌒, is placed first out of reverence (honorific transposition). ⧣ is the biliteral 'su', but it can also be an abbreviated form of 'nesu'. In full, the word for 'king' is ⧣⌒~, comprising ⧣ and ⌒ 'sut' or 'swt', meaning 'sedge' (the symbol of Upper Egypt: see page 97) and ~ (meaning 'of'). The word is sometimes transliterated as 'nesu', sometimes as 'nesut'. The fact that 'sut' is written first is thought possibly to be another example of honorific transposition.

The next part of the phrase is ⌂, which is the triliteral 'htp' (easier to pronounce as 'hotep' or 'hetep'). This is an abbreviation for 'offering', which is usually spelled out as ⌂⌐, comprising the triliteral 'htp' and two uniliterals for 't' and 'p' (acting here as phonetic complements to reinforce those letters in 'htp').

The final part of the phrase is △, which is the verb 'give'.

The name of one or more gods then follows, most commonly Osiris, ⫟⌐⧊ (see page 148), or Anubis, ⫯~☐ ⫰ (see page 136). Sometimes the god is mentioned instead of the king, as in ⫰△, 'hotep-di-inpu', meaning 'an offering that Anubis gives'.

Next comes ⫯⫯⫯, 'peret-kheru', which is a combination of ☐ (an abbreviation for 'going forth'), | (an abbreviation for 'voice'), and ◊◊ (an abbreviation for 'bread and beer', staple elements of the ancient Egyptian diet). Even though ⫯⫯⫯ is usually written with these bread and beer signs, the phrase is read simply as 'peret-kheru', which can be translated as 'voice offering' or 'invocation offering'. The precise meaning of this phrase is uncertain; it possibly refers to the person who is reciting the prayer. The phrase can also be written with ⌒ (a determinative used in words relating to bread and food) as 𓏏𓊪𓏌𓏌𓏌 ⌒.

It became more common to write the 'peret-kheru' phrase as 𓂞𓏏𓊪𓏌𓏌𓏌, 'di.f peret-kheru', 'so that he [that is, the god] may give an invocation offering'. ⌒ is 'give', the same verb written as 𓂊 in the 'hotep-di-nesu' formula mentioned above. ⌒ is used here as 'he', a singular masculine suffix pronoun added to the end of a word, and usually transliterated with a dot, as .f (see page 77). If there were several gods, this would become ⌒𓏭𓏤𓏤𓏤, 'di.sen', 'so that they may give'. 𓏭𓏤𓏤𓏤 (.sen) is the plural suffix pronoun for 'they' (see page 78).

The offerings are next listed, which can be the most extensive part of an inscription. Some are written in abbreviated form, most commonly 𓏊, 't', a word meaning 'bread' (and not the letter 't'), and 𓏊, 'henqet', meaning 'beer'. The bread and beer signs are not always included, but they may always have been intended by their inclusion in 𓏏𓊪𓏌𓏌𓏌.

Other offerings could include 𓃀, 'kau', meaning 'oxen'; 𓅿, 'apedu', meaning 'fowl'; 𓎯, 'shes', meaning 'alabaster' (probably alabaster oil jars); and 𓎟, 'menkhet', meaning 'cloth' or 'linen'. Often the offerings are accompanied by 𓆼, 'kha', 'one thousand', so a typical phrase could be 𓏏𓊪𓏌𓏌𓏌𓆼𓏊𓆼𓏊𓆼𓃀: an invocation offering of a thousand bread and beer and a thousand oxen and fowl.

The final part of such an inscription would be 𓈖𓂓𓈖, 'en ka en', 'for the ka [spirit] of', which is often followed by a description of the dead person as 𓄪𓅓, 'imakh', 'revered', then the dead person's name and then 𓊤, 'maa-kheru', 'the justified' (literally 'true of voice').

𓏶𓀁𓐍𓂝𓏏𓊵𓏏𓀔𓎟𓅓𓊨𓊨𓊨𓅓𓀭𓏏𓏏 would therefore read as: 'An offering that the king gives to Osiris, so that he may give a voice offering of 1,000 bread and beer, 1,000 oxen and fowl, for the ka of the revered one, Intef the justified'.

Finding Out More

The easiest way to find out more about hieroglyphs is to sign up for a college course or evening class. You can practise your hieroglyphs by visiting museum collections: a very large number of museums around the world have collections from Egypt. A visit to Egypt itself is also an incredible experience for seeing hieroglyphs, as they occur on virtually all the monuments and museum exhibits. The most convenient way to journey to the ancient sites is down the River Nile, and particularly for the first-time visitor an organised Nile cruise provides an excellent initiation.

Hundreds of books on Egypt are published each year, aimed at all levels of knowledge and all age groups. A selection of books is given here, but you are bound to come across others which may be just as attractive. There are also many websites devoted to numerous aspects of Egypt.

Hieroglyphs and Egypt in General. Packed with numerous entries, illustrations, plans, maps and reading references, the *British Museum Dictionary of Ancient Egypt* by Ian Shaw and Paul Nicholson (1995, British Museum Press) covers a whole range of topics. Another useful reference book is the *Atlas of Ancient Egypt* by John Baines and Jaromír Málek (1984, Phaidon), which is well illustrated and covers many elements of ancient Egypt, not just geography.

An introduction to aspects of the Egyptian language, including its various scripts, grammar and decipherment, is given in W.V. Davies, *Egyptian Hieroglyphs* (1987, British Museum Press), which is also reprinted in *Reading the Past. Ancient Writing from Cuneiform to the Alphabet*, introduced by J.T. Hooker (1990, British Museum Press).

To accompany an exhibition on the Rosetta Stone, the British Museum Press published *Cracking Codes. The Rosetta Stone and Decipherment* by Richard Parkinson (1999). Most of the book concentrates on the languages and scripts used throughout the history of ancient Egypt, with plenty of illustrated examples and detailed reading references.

Two books explain the meaning of a wide selection of hieroglyphs, in particular what the pictures represent, so they provide an excellent way of getting to know hieroglyphs and ancient Egyptian life: *Reading Egyptian Art. A Hieroglyphic Guide to Ancient Egyptian Painting and Sculpture* is by Richard H. Wilkinson (1992, Thames & Hudson); and *The Writings of Ancient Egypt* (English translation 1996, Abbeville Press) is by Maria Carmela Betrò (but be aware that the Gardiner numbers on pages 24–7 are wrong, but easily corrected, in this book, because the letter 'J' has been used, which Gardiner did not). These books are recommended for anyone with an interest in ancient Egypt, but particularly those who want an understanding of the significance of hieroglyphs but do not necessarily want to learn how to read them.

Another readable book by Richard H. Wilkinson is *Symbol & Magic in Egyptian Art* (1994, Thames & Hudson), which explains the symbolism of many aspects of ancient Egyptian life underlying art, including shape, colour, numbers and hieroglyphs.

Much recommended is *Papyrus* by Richard Parkinson and Stephen Quirke (1995, British Museum Press): not just about papyrus, this well-illustrated book contains a host of information on Egyptian writing, writing materials and hieratic.

Decipherment. *The Keys of Egypt. The Race to Read the Hieroglyphs* by Lesley and Roy Adkins (2000, HarperCollins) tells the exciting story of the decipherment of hieroglyphs by Jean-François Champollion, and his rivalry with Thomas Young. The book is also a readable introduction to Egypt and hieroglyphs, giving a glimpse of what Egypt and Egyptology was like in the early nineteenth century.

The Story of Decipherment. From Egyptian Hieroglyphs to Maya Script by Maurice Pope (revised edition 1999, Thames & Hudson) gives explanations of the decipherment of various ancient languages. The section on hieroglyphs includes a discussion of early attempts at decipherment up to the eighteenth century.

Learning the Language. The two most useful books for anyone wanting to study the language of hieroglyphs in any depth are the ones by Allen and Gardiner. *Middle Egyptian. An Introduction to the Language and Culture of Hieroglyphs* by James P. Allen (2000, Cambridge University Press) is an absolutely essential book for students, and gives up-to-date lessons on grammar, as well as explanations of all the hieroglyphs (following the Gardiner numbers) and a small but useful vocabulary.

The standard textbook for decades has been *Egyptian Grammar. Being an Introduction to the Study of Hieroglyphs* by Sir Alan Gardiner (1957, third edition, Griffith Institute, Oxford). The last 200 pages of this book (Gardiner's sign-list and extensive vocabulary) are the most useful for a student today. Although invaluable, this book should be used with caution, as some of it is out of date.

How To Read Egyptian Hieroglyphs. A Step-By-Step Guide to Teach Yourself by Mark Collier and Bill Manley (1998, British Museum Press) is also a good, up-to-date guide. Not as exhaustive as Allen's book (and therefore possibly less daunting for the beginner), it has one serious disadvantage: it does not use Gardiner numbers, but a different system that is confusingly similar to Gardiner numbers. It is therefore a 'stand-alone' book, which cannot easily be used alongside other reference books and dictionaries.

There is no comprehensive dictionary of hieroglyphs in English, but the best available short dictionary is *A Concise Dictionary of Middle Egyptian* by Raymond O. Faulkner (1962, Griffith Institute, Oxford). A very accessible dictionary for beginners, but in French, is *Petit Lexique de l'Egyptien hiéroglyphique à l'usage des débutants* by Bernadette Menu (1997, Geuthner).

There are two very recent, comprehensive dictionaries, but in German. *Die Sprache der Pharaonen: Grosses Handwörterbuch Ägyptisch-Deutsch (2800–950 v. Chr)* by Rainer Hannig (1995, Philipp von Zabern) is substantial and invaluable. Another in the same series is *Wortschatz der Pharaonen in Sachgruppen* by Rainer Hannig and Petra Vomberg (1998, Philipp von Zabern), a dictionary of words grouped by theme, such as 'Family and Life', 'Mathematics' and 'Metereology'.

Apart from a small English to Egyptian dictionary in Gardiner's book, there are no dictionaries that way round, except for *English-Egyptian Index of Faulkner's Concise Dictionary of Middle Egyptian* by David Shennum (1977, Undena Publications). This gives the English words in alphabetical order, then the transliterated Egyptian word, which in turn has to be looked up in Faulkner's dictionary to obtain the hieroglyphs.

Pharaohs. The only well-illustrated account of all pharaohs up to the Roman period is *Chronicle of the Pharaohs. The Reign-by-Reign Record of Rulers and Dynasties of Ancient Egypt* by Peter A. Clayton (1994, Thames & Hudson). In German a complete list of names is given in *Handbuch der ägyptischen Königsnamen* by Jürgen von Beckerath (revised edition 1999, von Zabern).

The types of names of the pharaohs, how they changed through history, and discussions of selected pharaohs with their cartouches are given in *Who Were the Pharaohs? A History of Their Names with a List of Cartouches* by Stephen Quirke (1990, British Museum Press).

Biographies of some of the pharaohs and other people are given in dictionary form, with reading references after each entry, in Michael Rice's *Who's Who in Ancient Egypt* (1999, Routledge).

A great deal on pharaohs can also be learned from the books listed below under 'Burial of the Dead', and biographies have also been published of some of the most famous pharaohs, such as Ramesses II.

Gods and Goddesses. A small but useful reference book is George Hart's *A Dictionary of Egyptian Gods and Goddesses* (1986, Routledge). Another small, illustrated dictionary is Manfred Lurker's *The Gods and Symbols of Ancient Egypt* (1980, Thames & Hudson), translated from his 1974 German book *Götter und Symbole der Alten Ägypter*.

The only comprehensive, readable book to deal with temples throughout Egypt is the highly illustrated *The Complete Temples of Ancient Egypt* by Richard H. Wilkinson (2000, Thames & Hudson).

Burial of the Dead. Essential reading is *Death and the Afterlife in Ancient Egypt* by John Taylor (2001, British Museum Press), fully illustrated in colour, and another useful book is *The Mummy in Ancient Egypt. Equipping the Dead for Eternity* by Salima Ikram and Aidan Dodson (1998, Thames & Hudson). Pyramids were burial places of the pharaohs and their family, and another essential and well-illustrated book is *The Complete Pyramids* by Mark Lehner (1997, Thames & Hudson).

A pharaoh-by-pharaoh guide to the tombs in the Valley of the Kings is the well-illustrated *The Complete Valley of the Kings. Tombs and Treasures of Egypt's Greatest Pharaohs* by Nicholas Reeves and Richard H. Wilkinson (1996, Thames & Hudson). Focusing on just one burial in the Valley of the Kings is the similarly well-illustrated *The Complete Tutankhamun* by Nicholas Reeves (1990, Thames & Hudson).

An up-to-date account of the tombs and temples of Thebes (including Valley of the Kings and Karnak) is *Thebes in Egypt. A Guide to the Tombs and Temples of Ancient Luxor* by Nigel and Helen Strudwick (1999, British Museum Press).

Guidebooks. There are many guidebooks to Egypt, but only two that give detailed descriptions of the ancient monuments for the visitor: *The Penguin Guide to Ancient Egypt* by William Murnane (revised edition 1996, Penguin) includes numerous maps and plans. *Blue Guide: Egypt* by Veronica Seton-Williams and Peter Stocks (3rd edition 1993, A & C Black/ WW Norton) is indispensable for visitors to the whole of Egypt, not just the ancient monuments.

Index